D0974186

GARY SOTO

NEW AND SELECTED POEMS

GARY SOTO

NEW AND SELECTED POEMS

CHRONICLE BOOKS
SAN FRANCISCO

Acknowledgments

Many of these poems were first published in literary magazines, most notably *Poetry*, which from 1974 to 1994 published fifty poems. *The Nation* also published fifteen during this period. Some of the new poems appeared in *The Colorado Review, The Michigan Quarterly, The Nation, Ontario Review, Ploughshares, Poetry, Prairie Schooner,* and *The Threepenny Review.*

The author wishes to thank Christopher Buckley, Jon Veinberg, and the late Ernesto Trejo – steady friends.

This book is for Carolyn – love in all kinds of weather.

Printed in the United States.

Book and cover design: Michael Osborne Design
Cover illustration: José Ortega

Library of Congress Cataloging-in-Publication Data available.

ISBN: 0-8118-0758-4 (pbk)
          0-8118-0761-4 (hc)

Distributed in Canada by Raincoast Books,
8680 Cambie Street, Vancouver, B.C. V6P 6M9

10 9 8 7 6 5 4 3 2 1

Chronicle Books
275 Fifth Street
San Francisco, CA 94103

CONTENTS

I was really little more than a boy when I first scribbled out a few sad lines of poetry in my apartment, which I shared with my brother Rick, an artist, and a few other roommates, also artists and college students. We were poor as sparrows picking at the free fruits of the valley. Having come from a family with no books, I didn't know better. I didn't know the continuity of ancient literature, the mechanics of writing, or the mesmerizing effect poetry can have on its readers. I knew the "beat poets," who amazed me by their audacity to shrug off the world, and I thought their wildness should stampede through my hometown, Fresno. What would be better than to rant from our second-story apartment on Weldon Avenue, within earshot of my beautiful neighbor, Carolyn, brushing her hair in the sunlight and teasing this boy into action. I would serenade her with my first poems, marry her, and stay with her for as many years as I had been single. I felt happy in this apartment and taken by the haunting sounds that trembled through the walls – the train tracks ran so close to our apartment that we could open a window in the dining room and toss an orange at the locomotive and its freight click-clacking over the rails. We did this occasionally, but more often than not we sat around the apartment opening and closing the refrigerator, certain that eventually, miraculously, something delicious would appear.

Suffering through college poverty, my brother Rick and I accepted all kinds of odd jobs, including waking before dawn to take the labor bus from Chinatown to chop beets or cotton. Or we collected aluminum, pushed mowers, shoveled weeds, washed cars, picked grapes – anything to get by. But to survive the boredom and loneliness in a town where the worse you felt the worse you were treated, I was reading poetry that friends suggested, given over to the destiny of poverty, unmanageable and angry in my ragged Levis.

I decided I wasn't going to grovel for a job. I gave up buying new clothes, for instance, and my hair was wild on my shoulders. I believed in César Chávez and the United Farm Workers. I believed in fasting and not eating meat. I believed in drinking water, the only fluid I accepted in my body. I believed in walking and paying homage to the dusty ruins of Fresno, namely every beautiful house that was torn

1

down by our City Fathers in the name of Urban Renewal. I had given up an array of social conventions, including Catholicism, which I would later embrace as salvation, and given myself over to the alchemy of poetry. By early 1973, I was devouring contemporary Ameri-can poetry and Latin American poetry, a literary border crossing that I couldn't fathom. Reading Pablo Neruda, I was fascinated by his energy and the lush, occasionally surrealistic landscapes. I was bewildered by what must have been the godly permission this poet received to write so strangely. I wanted such permission, too. There was nothing to match Neruda's marvelous vision, and when I first glimpsed a photo-graph of him on the back of a book, he reminded me of Picasso, the "other" Pablo, both with frighteningly large and luminous eyes.

My brother and I had arrived at college in a squeaky VW bug with-out having read more than the backs of milk cartons and cereal boxes. A timid writer, I gazed over my meager poems in fear of grammatical glitches. I chewed my fingernails to bloody nubs, worried that solving the proper use of the subjunctive was more like high math than art. But by summer 1973, after my fear of writing poorly had disappeared, I knew my pulse was timed to the heart of this valley. The conversion to a real subject was sudden and a result, I believed ignorantly, of boarding my first jet airliner and looking down at the shimmer of the valley. Within a two-week period I wrote the sequence "The Elements of San Joaquin" and also poems for my father, dead many years – poems like "Braly Street," "The Evening of Ants," "Spirit," and "Photo, 1957," among others.

I remember writing "Spirit" while I was in Carolyn's apartment. It was midday, and flies were banging against the window. As the deep wailing inside me surfaced, I began to compose with a pencil (then moved quickly to the typewriter, my mode of operation for years) a linear poem about a jealous father returning for his now-married widow. More specifically, this poem evokes an image of my grand-mother discovering in her cupboard a pile of cemetery grass clippings two days after my father's death. There is also a haunting reference to the furniture moving, however slightly, into different positions. This poem literally scared me out of the apartment. Shaken, I remember walking down Weldon Street to see another poet, Larry Sparks, who was living his poor life in a Quonset hut. He was frying potatoes, his only meal for the day, and I remember the plate he served me – potatoes with a watery string of onions. It was the meal of poets.

Having literally no place to go, I haunted the ruins of Braly Street, where our house was torn down, an area that was almost all Mexican. Some of the families were still there, having given up the deeds of their houses but homesteading, thus fighting the city's planned eviction. This was south Fresno, where there were plans to bulldoze our barrio and make room for an industrial park. Nothing of the sort was constructed, and the good people of Fresno remember this. To this day there are empty lots choked with weeds and rubble and the meanderings of stray cats. This place, this emptiness, and these few totems of the past haunt me and have shaped my work and its sense of loss. At dusk, in this desolate place, the sun throws out to me a yellowish light, a sort of "end-of-the-world color."

I began writing my first poems in 1973, and soon fell in with the poets in Fresno – Leonard Adame, Omar Salinas, Ernesto Trejo, and Jon Veinberg. We were all wrestling with words and arguing over silly and large matters, including how we should barter our poems. We knew the exchange would be just, that is, the exchange of our poems for some bread and fatty meat, but in this no-nonsense valley who would listen to such notions. We laughed at ourselves and celebrated our brotherhood in back yards where on extravagant nights we ate barbecued chicken and drank quarts of beer. Except for Jon, we were all Chicanos and, determined to realize our talents, we settled in for the long haul. We trusted our instincts and wrote poems that first appeared in college magazines. Then, as young poets will do, we got gutsy. We licked stamps and sent out poems because we wanted to be published, just as our teachers were published, in literary magazines. We were on our way on this gray and rusty tanker called Poetry. We saluted ourselves and thought nothing of it when once, at a poetry reading, the moderator, himself a Chicano in rags, whimsically introduced us with a wave of his hand, "I knew these guys when they were eating orange peels for a living."

We were young and making up poems at the beginning of the 1970s. Now it's the mid-1990s and I'm tinkering with "Waterwheel," one of the last poems to go into the new section. In the poem I'm five and sitting in dirt. A rain has passed, and so have the men who worked at Sun-Maid Raisin, my father among them. I'm waiting for a friend to show up, as he promised, and offer me a clam shell with a scene of an ancient Chinese water wheel, which I could turn with my thumb and pass the season with. The poem, I suppose, is about longing and the arrival of beauty from a long journey, wet with clouds and speaking a language that makes my eyes spin. For me, that beauty happened in the form of my wife, Carolyn, almost always the first reader of my poetry. Then came the cantankerous but generous bellowing of my second reader, poet Christopher Buckley. Finally, I have been blessed with friends, among them the above-mentioned gang of four, one of whom we have already lost to death. For that brother, Ernesto, I wrote many of these poems. Even in my first poor efforts, and in the crazy world behind my eyes, he was a tree with flowing hair, rooted in family. It was for Ernesto and his passing that I wrote, "the work of its roots bore down through rock/And darkness, all for the apparent flow of youth."

THE ELEMENTS OF SAN JOAQUIN

THE ELEMENTS OF SAN JOAQUIN
for César Chávez

Field

The wind sprays pale dirt into my mouth
The small, almost invisible scars
On my hands.

The pores in my throat and elbows
Have taken in a seed of dirt of their own.

After a day in the grape fields near Rolinda
A fine silt, washed by sweat,
Has settled into the lines
On my wrists and palms.

Already I am becoming the valley,
A soil that sprouts nothing.
For any of us.

Wind

A dry wind over the valley
Peeled mountains, grain by grain,
To small slopes, loose dirt
Where red ants tunnel.

The wind strokes
The skulls and spines of cattle
To white dust, to nothing,

Covers the spiked tracks of beetles,
Of tumbleweed, of sparrows
That pecked the ground for insects.

Evenings, when I am in the yard weeding,
The wind picks up the breath of my armpits

Like dust, swirls it
Miles away

And drops it
On the ear of a rabid dog,
And I take on another life.

Wind

When you got up this morning the sun
Blazed an hour in the sky,

A lizard hid
Under the curled leaves of manzanita
And winked its dark lids.

Later, the sky grayed,
And the cold wind you breathed
Was moving under your skin and already far
From the small hives of your lungs.

Stars

At dusk the first stars appear.
Not one eager finger points toward them.
A little later the stars spread with the night
And an orange moon rises
To lead them, like a shepherd, toward dawn.

Sun

In June the sun is a bonnet of light
Coming up,
Little by little,
From behind a skyline of pine.

The pastures sway with fiddle-neck,
Tassels of foxtail.

At Piedra
A couple fish on the river's edge,
Their shadows deep against the water.
Above, in the stubbled slopes,
Cows climb down
As the heat rises
In a mist of blond locusts,
Returning to the valley.

Rain

When autumn rains flatten sycamore leaves,
The tiny volcanos of dirt
Ants raised around their holes,
I should be out of work.

My silverware and stack of plates will go unused
Like the old, my two good slacks
Will smother under a growth of lint
And smell of the old dust
That rises
When the closet door opens or closes.

The skin of my belly will tighten like a belt
And there will be no reason for pockets.

Harvest

East of the sun's slant, in the vineyard that never failed,
A wind crossed my face, moving the dust
And a portion of my voice a step closer to a new year.

The sky went black in the ninth hour of rolling trays,
And in the distance ropes of rain dropped to pull me
From the thick harvest that was not mine.

Fog

If you go to your window
You will notice a fog drifting in.

The sun is no stronger than a flashlight.
Not all the sweaters
Hung in closets all summer

Could soak up this mist. The fog:
A mouth nibbling everything to its origin,
Pomegranate trees, stolen bicycles,

The string of lights at a used-car lot,
A Pontiac with scorched valves.

In Fresno the fog is passing
The young thief prying a window screen,
Graying my hair that falls
And goes unfound, my fingerprints
Slowly growing a fur of dust –

One hundred years from now
There should be no reason to believe
I lived.

Daybreak

In this moment when the light starts up
In the east and rubs
The horizon until it catches fire,

We enter the fields to hoe,
Row after row, among the small flags of onion,
Waving off the dragonflies
That ladder the air.

And tears the onions raise
Do not begin in your eyes but in ours,
In the salt blown
From one blister into another;

They begin in knowing
You will never waken to bear
The hour timed to a heart beat,
The wind pressing us closer to the ground.

When the season ends,
And the onions are unplugged from their sleep,
We won't forget what you failed to see,
And nothing will heal
Under the rain's broken fingers.

SUMMER

Once again, tell me, what was it like?
There was a windowsill of flies.
It meant the moon pulled its own weight
And the black sky cleared itself
Like a sneeze.

What about the farm worker?
He had no bedroom. He had a warehouse
Of heat, a swamp cooler
That turned no faster than a raffle cage.

And the farms?
There were groves
Of fig trees that went unpicked.
The fruit wrinkled and flattened
Like the elbows
Of an old woman.

What about the Projects in the Eastside?
I can't really say. Maybe a child
Burned his first book of matches.
Maybe the burn is disappearing
Under the first layer
Of skin.

And next summer?
It will be the same. Boredom,
In early June, will settle
On the eyelash shading your pupil from dust,
On the shoulder you look over
To find the sun rising
From the Sierras.

FIELD POEM

When the foreman whistled
My brother and I
Shouldered our hoes,
Leaving the field.
We returned to the bus
Speaking
In broken English, in broken Spanish
The restaurant food,
The tickets to a dance
We wouldn't buy with our pay.

From the smashed bus window,
I saw the leaves of cotton plants
Like small hands waving good-bye.

HOEING

During March while hoeing long rows
Of cotton
Dirt lifted in the air
Entering my nostrils
And eyes
The yellow under my fingernails

The hoe swung
Across my shadow   chopping weeds
And thick caterpillars
That shriveled
Into rings
And went where the wind went

When the sun was on the left
And against my face
Sweat   the sea
That is still within me
Rose and fell from my chin
Touching land
For the first time

AVOCADO LAKE

A body moves under the dark lake —
The throat is a tube of water, the hands
Are those of a child reaching for his mother.
It may be hours before the body rises
To the surface.

It is even longer before the body is found.
To blow breath in him is useless —
The lungs need to be wrung like sponge.

The gray film peeled like tape from the eyes.
The curled fingers rubbed and kissed.

And now, at daybreak, the willows
Once again hold the heat, and a young girl,
On the shore where a friend has gone under,
Skims pebbles across the lake,
Over what remains of him –
His phlegm drifts beneath the surface,
As his life did.

THE MORNING THEY SHOT TONY LOPEZ, BARBER AND PUSHER WHO WENT TOO FAR, 1958

When they entered through the back door,
You were too slow in raising an arm
Or thinking of your eyes refusing the light,
Or your new boots moored under the bed,
Or your wallet on the bureau, open
And choking with bills,
Or your pockets turned inside out, hanging breathless as tongues,
Or the vendor clearing his throat in the street,
Or your watch passed on to another's son,
Or the train to Los Banos,
The earth you would slip into like a shirt
And drift through forever.
When they entered, and shot once,
You twisted the face your mother gave
With the three, short grunts that let you slide
In the same blood you closed your eyes to.

TELEPHONING GOD
for Jon Veinberg

Drunk in the kitchen, I ring God

And get Wichita,
Agatha drunk and on the bed's edge, undoing
Her bra.

Dial again, and Topeka comes through like snoring,
Though no one sleeps. Not little Jennifer
Yelling "But Mommy,"
                              nor Ernie kissing
The inside of his wrist, whispering
"This is a Gorgeous Evening."

Dial again, and only the sound of spoons crashing
In a cafeteria in Idaho,

A little silence, then a gnat circling the ear
Of Angela beaten and naked in the vineyard,
Her white legs glowing.

IN DECEMBER

The dogs, the spotted dogs,
Fenced and barking,
Remain with me –
And the old face
Of a midget carting groceries
And muttering a rosary.

From town I went south,
Beyond the new
Freeway, searching.
In one house on Sarah Street

14

A doll's head,
Her nose chipped,
Facing the bedroom –
A broom was in there
But the floor was unswept.
If there was wind
The puffs of black lint
Would have rolled
Like a tumbleweed
Toward their own
Particular deaths.
In the kitchen a draft
Moved like a housewife,
Reaching into the cupboards
To find nothing
But vinegar
And an unstrung necklace
Of dead flies.

So long ago
The yard was gardened –
Tomatoes hanging
Like small red globes
And carrots poking
Into the kennel of earth;
On the line clothes lifted
With a slight wind.
And a child, perhaps,
Shaded by a cottonwood
And nailing on nailed two-by-fours
Or burning a shoe box
Imagines a hotel
And a lobby of people
Wanting out.

When I started home
Darkness was gliding west –
In a thin sycamore

Whose branches pointed
To a few stars,
Nests showed against the sky
And I felt a deepening
Like the night
Not yet an hour old.

COPPER

Leonard's wallet yawned open
And toothless, and the morning
Coughed from an empty shelf.
We walked dirt alleys after mass,
Collecting copper.
In the gravel yard, near the tracks,
We yanked out wire from the dashboards
Of buckled trucks, coiled tubing
And the short-throated pipes
Furred in oil. After selling
On the Westside, we went home
And napped where there was shade.

Today we are bloated on beer,
Glowing before a snowy TV.
Outside, snow slants into the street.
We laugh at nights we slept
Cold, in coats,
And I hugged a cat
That smelled like a broom —
Slugs laced the floor with silver.
If it were warm outside or we drunker
And swearing in the name of Christ
Or the Connie tattooed on Leonard's arm,
We would pick through an alley
Until we spotted the soft glow

Of copper, the only light needed
To show the way back.

HISTORY

Grandma lit the stove.
Morning sunlight
Lengthened in spears
Across the linoleum floor.
Wrapped in a shawl,
Her eyes small
With sleep,
She sliced *papas,*
Pounded chiles
With a stone
Brought from Guadalajara.

                          After
Grandpa left for work,
She hosed down
The walk her sons paved
And in the shade
Of a chinaberry,
Unearthed her
Secret cigar box
Of bright coins
And bills, counted them
In English,
Then in Spanish,
And buried them elsewhere.
Later, back
From the market,
Where no one saw her,
She pulled out
Pepper and beet, spines

Of asparagus
From her blouse,
Tiny chocolates
From under a paisley bandana,
And smiled.

That was the fifties
And Grandma in her fifties,
A face streaked
From cutting grapes
And boxing plums.
I remember her insides
Were washed of tapeworm,
Her arms swelled into knobs
Of small growths –
Her second son
Dropped from a ladder
And was dust.
And yet I do not know
The sorrows
That sent her praying
In the dark of a closet,
The tear that fell
At night
When she touched loose skin
Of belly and breasts.
I do not know why
Her face shines
Or what goes beyond this shine,
Only the stories
That pulled her
From Taxco to San Joaquin,
Delano to Westside,
The places
In which we all begin.

MOVING AWAY

Remember that we are moving away   brother
From those years
In the same house with a white stepfather
What troubled him has been forgotten

But what troubled us has settled
Like dirt
In the nests of our knuckles
And cannot be washed away

All those times you woke shivering
In the night
From a coldness I
Could not understand
And cupped a crucifix beneath the covers

All those summers we hoed our yard
In the afternoon sun
The heat waving across our faces
And we waved back wasps
While the one we hated
Watched us from under a tree and said nothing

We will remember those moments   brother

And now that we are far
From one another
What I want to speak of
Is the quiet of a room just before a daybreak
And you next to me   sleeping

MOVING AWAY

Remember that you are moving away   sister
From what was a summer
Of hunger
And of thorns deep in your feet
Prayers that unraveled
Like mama's stockings
At the day's end
When she came back from candling eggs

Those small things you knew on the old street
Have vanished   a holly bush
And its bright jays
The rocks you scratched
From the yard
And were your dolls   blond dolls
Given heartbeats   names   legs
The sighs of those
About to cry
                    Remember that you have left
Grandpa nodding like a tall weed
Over his patch of chilies and tomatoes
Left a jar of secrets
Buried in the vacant lot
On a hot day
And our family some distance
From your life
Remember

SPIRIT

When Grandma cried
Hugging the shirt
You stood in the room again

You saw her drop
To her knees
Kiss the rosary
And repeat prayers
Until a white paste
Gathered in the corners
Of her mouth
The next morning
Your cup and plate
Brimmed with cemetery grass
And the sofa
You gave Grandpa
Turned and faced south
We know you came back father
And in the doorway
Leading to your bedroom
Wanted to fog
The family's photo
With the breath
You did not have
And years later
When your wife slept
With another
You waited
At their feet
Until they turned
From one another
Eyes closed
And sighing
Leaving them
A cupboard opened
The garage light
On and burning silent
As your jealousy
But was it you father
Who sent me across
A dry orchard

Where I pointed
To a thin cloud
And thought
Beyond
That cloud
You lived in Limbo
God's Limbo
And were watching
And soon   for
The first time
You would come to me
Calling   *son   son*

PHOTO, 1957

In the one torn
Where your waist begins
You hold Debra
And look up,
Smiling to a cloud perhaps
Or a silver blimp
Pushing slowly against
The March wind.
You are twenty-two,
My age now,
Your hair curled upward
Into a hive your
Man enters, your eyes
Twin pinpoints of light.
You do not know
In a few months
You will waken alone
And where
The rooms go unlighted,
It will be cold.

At dusk
The shadows of brooms
And backless chairs
Will pull southward,
Pointing the way
The dead vanish.
Then the house
Will tick like fire,
The cat circle
A table and refuse to lie
Flat, and in the yard
I will salt the slugs
Trailing the rain.

THE EVENING OF ANTS

I climbed into the chinaberry
With a play telephone
Rang for a taxi
To drive me away
And for a man to tighten
The leaky pipes
That shivered like our dogs
I rang mama
And hung up on her
Giggled   called again
To tell her I was hungry

Across a dirt yard
Chickens pecked at the broken glass
Winking with sunlight
And the Italian
Who would roll his Packard
A month later
Was alone on his porch talking

Hours passed   birds passed
And those orange cats
Who eventually dropped
Under car tires
Moved as their shade moved

                    Evening neared
And the moment our father slipped
From a ladder   our mother
Reached the door
That opened into a white room
A white nurse   It was the moment
I came down from the tree
And into our house
Where a leash of ants
Swarmed for the rice   the cupboards   the stove
Carrying off what there was to carry
Between one root and the next

BRALY STREET

Every summer
The asphalt softens
Giving under the edge
Of boot heels and the trucks
That caught radiators
Of butterflies.
Bottle caps and glass
Of the forties and fifties
Hold their breath
Under the black earth
Of asphalt and are silent
Like the dead whose mouths
Have eaten dirt and bermuda.
Every summer I come

To this street
Where I discovered ants bit,
Matches flare,
And pinto beans unraveled
Into plants; discovered
Aspirin will not cure a dog
Whose fur twitches.

It's sixteen years
Since our house
Was bulldozed and my father
Stunned into a coma ...
Where it was,
An oasis of chickweed
And foxtails.
Where the almond tree stood
There are wine bottles
Whose history
Is a liver. The long caravan
Of my uncle's footprints
Has been paved
With dirt. Where my father
Cemented a pond
There is a cavern of red ants
Living on the seeds
The wind brings
And cats that come here
To die among
The browning sage.

It's sixteen years
Since bottle collectors
Shoveled around
The foundation
And the almond tree
Opened its last fruit
To the summer.

The houses are gone,
The Molinas, Morenos,
The Japanese families
Are gone, the Okies gone
Who moved out at night
Under a canopy of
Moving stars.

In '57 I sat
On the porch, salting
Slugs that came out
After the rain,
While inside my uncle
Weakened with cancer
And the blurred vision
Of his hands
Darkening to earth.
In '58 I knelt
Before my father
Whose spine was pulled loose.
Before his face still
Growing a chin of hair,
Before the procession
Of stitches behind
His neck, I knelt
And did not understand.

Braly Street is now
Tin ventilators
On the warehouses, turning
Our sweat
Toward the yellowing sky;
Acetylene welders
Beading manifolds,
Stinging the half-globes
Of retinas. When I come
To where our house was,

I come to weeds
And a sewer line tied off
Like an umbilical cord;
To the chinaberry
Not pulled down
And to its rings
My father and uncle
Would equal, if alive.

FROM

THE TALE OF SUNLIGHT

THE LITTLE ONES

When fog
Stands weed-high
And sky
Is the color
Of old bed sheets,
Molina and I
Squat under an oak
On a bench of roots,
Burning paper
And leaves
To keep warm.
We blow into
Our hands
And the white
That comes out
Drifts upward
Where heat
Does not reach.
Our eyes glow
Before the fire,
And Molina says
The sparrows
In this tree,
The little ones,
Find their heaven
Where the sky
Meets the earth.
For days
They will point
Far into coldness
Until that cold
Becomes the dark
Blowing across
Their eyes.
They will know
The South

When a bundle of smoke
Moves against
The wind
And fields lift
The rains
Of a thousand years.

.

THE SOUP

The lights off, the clock glowing 2:10,
And Molina is at the table drawing what he thinks is soup
And its carrots rising through a gray broth.

He adds meat and peppers it with pencil markings.
The onion has gathered the peas in its smile.
The surface is blurred with the cold oils squeezed from a lime.

He adds hominy and potato that bob
In a current of pork fat, from one rim to the other,
Crashing into the celery that has canoed such a long way.

Spoon handle that is a plank an ant climbs.
Saucer that is the slipped disk of a longhorn.
Napkin that is shredded into a cupful of snow.

SONG FOR THE POCKETS

They carry the spoon that unearthed another tin spoon,
A magnet furred in iron filings,
A shag of lint.

They carry fiddle-neck and the arrow-face foxtail,
A harmonica grinning with rust.
The salt that forgot the palm it was rubbed from.

They carry the key whose door was burned,
A rattle of seeds capsuled in foil —
All that was lost in the street raised by its own rules.

THE SHEPHERD
for Ernesto Trejo

The grasses begin where he begins
The descent home,
A harp swung over his left shoulder,
The moon over the other.
At his waist, a small satchel
Of jicama and a long nostril of turnip.

Kin to the felled tree,
The collapsed stone,
The three-legged chicken pickled and showing
In a cellar of the poor,
He is returning at
The pace at which the sun untangles itself

By the moon's laughter
The willow's desire to touch its feet.
There is no hurry, toss the trees.
Good Wood, Good Fire, fall the chinked coins of leaves.
Where he steps, the grasses rub
Their notched faces, whispering his name.

THE FIRST

After the river
Gloved its fingers
With leaves

And the autumn sunlight
Spoked the earth
Into two parts,
The villagers undid
Their houses,
Thatch by thatch,
And unplucked
The stick fences
That held grief
And leaned from the wind
That swung their way.
What the sun raised –
Squash and pumpkin,
Maize collared
In a white fungus –
They left, for the earth
Was not as it was
Remembered, the iguana
Being stretched
Into belts
The beaver curling
Into handbags;
Their lakes bruised
Gray with smoke
That unraveled from cities.
Clearing a path
Through the forest,
A path that closed
Behind them
As the day opened
A smudge of its blue,
They were the first
To leave, unnoticed,
Without words,
For it no longer
Mattered to say
The world was once blue.

Bloated on beans, squash,
Goat's milk, I left
Before dawn for Taxco
With a clock
Needing a new face
And God knows what.
I followed the river Calabaza
Brimming with weeds
And lizards
Until it stopped
Where stones climbed
Like a stairway
These terrible hills.
At noon, or close to noon,
The heat rising
To the level of the wind,
I saw an iguana flutter
From under a bush
And vanish into the ribs
Of a fleshless mule.
The crazy thing was smiling.
It is the truth, friend.
When I picked up the ribs,
Turned it over, shook
It like a child,
The iguana did not appear
Or even click its tongue.
So I went on, did not
Look back, but thought
That God was testing me.
I could expect a bush
To flare before my eyes
And the umbilical cords
Of the newly born,
Pigeons to choke

In the noose
Of their own breathing
And fall from the trees.
So this was the world, at noon.

AT THE CANTINA

In the cantina
Of six tables
A woman fingers
The ear lobe
Of a bank teller.
It is late,
And this place is empty
As a crushed hat.
A galaxy of flies
Circles the lamp.
Manuel wipes the counter,
Flicking ashes
Onto the floor.
The voices of
That couple
With the faces of oxen
On a hot day
Reach over his shoulder
And vanish
Into the mirror.
Finally they leave
Without nodding good-bye,
His hand on
Her right breast,
Her thumb hooked
In his watch pocket.
Manuel locks up,
Uncorks a bottle

And sits at a table.
All night he drinks
And his hands fold
And unfold,
Against the light,
A kingdom of animal shadows –
The Jackal,
The Hummingbird,
The sleepy-eyed Llama,
An Iguana munching air –
While the rooster stretches
To the day not there yet.

THE CREATURE

This morning something
Perched like a bird
On my left shoulder,
And was silent.
If I brushed it away,
It reappeared
Like a premonition.
If I ran,
It clawed deep
Into my coat,
My wool coat,
And closed its eyes –
Or what I thought
Were its eyes.
So, here I was
Walking the town
Perplexed like a priest,
My neck stiff
As a new beard,
And no friend

Waving ¡Hola!
That afternoon
I prayed and lit
A candle for the spirit
Of my wife
Dead two years,
And still this
Creature tightened
And yawned
Into my ear.
At supper in my room,
It ate my bread
And the handle
Of a sharp knife.
To that I said Enough!
And left hatless
For the cantina,
Where again the creature
Lay on my shoulder
Like the hand of someone
Bearing grief.

A FEW COINS

Now and then
Manuel, stunned with
The same boredom
Of an ant circling
A dirty spoon,
Has visions of wealth.
Say, for instance,
To form a circus:
Nude dancers, a midget
With minute genitals,
Monkeys boxing

For carrots,
All the ugly gathered
Under one tent.
The prize attraction
Is a rooster
With the command
Of several dozen words,
A Latin phrase or two.
Or last week
After a conversation
With a shovel,
He wanted to bottle urine
And peddle it
To the tourists
In Taxco, saying
It is the lake water
In which Virgin Olga bathed ...
Sometimes he brags
He worked outside Toluca
For Americanos,
Shoveling stones
Into boxes.
One morning
He unearthed a salamander
Cut from bone, collared
With small holes
Where jewels shone.
He sold it
To a skinny gringo,
And in parting
With it, wept
And muttered like
A harelipped prophet –
Bird in the stupid tree,
Wink at me ...
God above the tree,
Call me Manuel the genius –
And simply walked away.

CATALINA TREVIÑO IS REALLY FROM HEAVEN

Last night
At Mother Tomas's,
We danced the
Chicken-with-its-head-chopped-off,
Her hands on my buttocks,
My crotch puffed
Like a lung
And holding its breath.
This wonderful woman
Stitched my neck
With kisses
And told secrets —
The silverware she stole,
Her spinster aunt
Living in Taxco, a former lover
With a heart condition.
I in turn, being educated
And a man of
Absolutely no wealth,
Whispered a line
Of bad poetry
And bit her left earlobe.
Afterward we left
Arm in arm
For my room, for our clothes
Piled in a chair, and she
Fingering my bellybutton,
I opening her
Like a large Bible,
The kingdom of hair.

Sweeping the floor
I find a ring
Caught in a tiny bush
Of lint and hair,
A ring with no inscription
Or stone. However
It is gold
And could belong
To the grinning one
Who left
With two women,
Two bottles of mescal,
A headache that
Will arrive
With the mail
And his wife striking
Him with a chair.
And there is some
Possibility
It fell from
The finger of
The ditch keeper
Or the old one
Who peeks through keyholes.
I do not rule out
The odds
It belongs to the retired sergeant
Who danced alone,
Went home alone
And kissed his arm goodnight.
No matter, no matter,
It is gold
I shall sell
To the dentist.
Perhaps he will press it

Into the barber's
Two good molars
Or the chipped eyetooth
Of the widow
Who will again smile,
Drink late,
And shine with
What fire shines
Inside her.

THE TALE OF SUNLIGHT

Listen, nephew.
When I opened the cantina
At noon
A triangle of sunlight
Was stretched out
On the floor
Like a rug
Like a tired cat.
It flared in
From the window
Through a small hole
Shaped like a yawn.
Strange I thought
And placed my hand
Before the opening,
But the sunlight
Did not vanish.
I pulled back
The shutters
And the room glowed,
But this pyramid
Of whiteness
Was simply brighter.

The sunlight around it
Appeared soiled
Like the bed sheet
Of a *borracho.*
Amazed, I locked the door,
Closed the windows.
Workers, in from
The fields, knocked
To be let in,
Children peeked
Through the shutters,
But I remained silent.
I poured a beer,
At a table
Shuffled a pack
Of old cards,
And watched it
Cross the floor,
Hang on the wall
Like a portrait
Like a calendar
Without numbers.
When a fly settled
In the sunlight
And disappeared
In a wreath of smoke,
I tapped it with the broom,
Spat on it.
The broom vanished.
The spit sizzled.
It is the truth, little one.
I stood eye to blank eye
And by misfortune
This finger
This pink stump
Entered the sunlight,
Snapped off

With a dry sneeze,
And fell to the floor
As a gift
To the ants
Who know me
For what I gave.

THE SPACE

West of town,
Near Hermosa's well,
I sleep sometimes –
In a hammock of course –
Among avocado trees,
Cane, spider-grass,
The hatchet-faced *chula,*
The banana's umbrella
Of leaves.
It is here
In the spiny brush
Where cocks gabble,
Where the javelina
Lies on its side
Like an overturned high-heel.
I say it is enough
To be where the smells
Of creatures
Braid like rope
And to know if
The grasses rustle
It is only
A lizard passing.
It is enough, brother,
Listening to a bird coo
A leash of parables,

Keeping an eye
On the moon,
The space
Between cork trees
Where the sun first appears.

WHERE SPARROWS WORK HARD

THE STREET

Not far
From the cat dropped
By a .22, among
The slouched weeds
Of South Fresno,
Or the old janitor
Pasting bottle caps
Into a scrapbook,
Prieta is a five-year-old
At the kitchen table
Coloring a portrait
Of God, in the blank face
Of a frying pan.

She rings his eyes
Green, beards his chin
In fire, crowns
His head with a halo
That is little more
Than a dinner plate,
Little less
Than the hubcap
Wheeling free
Over the deep ruts
In Malaga.

Where his hands
Reach out, offering
A flower hooded
In the approximate light,
There is scribbling
She tries to undo
With an eraser
And a string of spit.
It never looks right.

•

The shade
Of the back porch,
And Uncle is doing push-ups
On his fists,
His dog tags ticking
Against the cement
Each time he goes down.
When the cat comes
Near, he spits and she steps back
To sniff the air
For the rat who nibbles
Dropped popcorn
In the presence of a broom.
Or it is perhaps the hen
Locked behind wire
Whose filth will scatter
When her neck
Is a loose tube
Of feathers
And her claws
Quiet into roots.

•

Grandma shuffles
From one fruit tree
To the next, her hands
Skinned with dirt,
Her breathing
A hive of gnats.
She is Indian,
My brother believes,
And lassoes her
To a fence
With the rope

That pulled a cow
To its death,
A sow to market,
A piano
To the third floor
Sparrows circling
As it rose
Past an arena of trees.

Poverty is a pair
Of boots, rain,
Twin holsters slapping
His side, and a hand
Cocked into a pistol.
When he points
And the smoke lifts,
She is gone
In the notch
He scratches into his wrist.

•

I'm the child
In a chinaberry
Flicking matches
Into a jar of flies, wingless
And frisking
Themselves empty.
The lid closed,
Smoke knots and unknots
From the hole I poked
So they can breathe.
I shake them,
And they are a raffle
For the ants,
A small cargo
For the wind

To haul into the smeared
Ash of evening.

This will be hours later.
For now, the sun breaks
Above the houses,
Lifting the shadows
On their scaffolds.
A car rattles
From the drive
And stalls in
A great sigh of steam.
I see this and note
That when someone calls
No one has to go.

MISSION TIRE FACTORY, 1969

All through lunch Peter pinched at his crotch,
And Jesús talked about his tattoos,
And I let the flies crawl my arm, undisturbed,
Thinking it was wrong, a buck sixty-five,
The wash of rubber in our lungs,
The ovens we would enter, squinting
– because earlier in the day Manny fell
From his machine, and when we carried him
To the workshed (blood from
Under his shirt, in his pants)
All he could manage, in an ignorance
Outdone only by pain, was to take three dollars
From his wallet, and say:
"Buy some sandwiches. You guys saved my life."

TV IN BLACK AND WHITE

In the mid-sixties
We were sentenced to watch
The rich on TV – Donna Reed
High-heeled in the kitchen,
Ozzie Nelson bending
In his eighth season, over golf.
While he swung, we hoed
Fields flagged with cotton
Because we understood a sock
Should have a foot,
A cuff a wrist,
And a cup was always
Smaller than the thirst.
When Donna turned
The steak and onions,
We turned grape trays
In a vineyard
That we worked like an abacus,
A row at a time.

And today the world
Still plots, unravels with
Piano lessons for this child,
Braces for that one –
Gin in the afternoon,
Ice from the bucket ...
But if the electricity
Fails, in this town,
A storefront might
Be smashed, sacks may find
Hands, a whistle
Point the way.
And if someone steps out
With a black and white TV,
It's because we love you Donna,
We miss you Ozzie.

MEXICANS BEGIN JOGGING

At the factory I worked
In the fleck of rubber, under the press
Of an oven yellow with flame,
Until the border patrol opened
Their vans and my boss waved for us to run.
"Over the fence, Soto," he shouted,
And I shouted that I was American.
"No time for lies," he said, and pressed
A dollar in my palm, hurrying me
Through the back door.

Since I was on his time, I ran
And became the wag to a short tail of Mexicans –
Ran past the amazed crowds that lined
The street and blurred like photographs, in rain.
I ran from that industrial road to the soft
Houses where people paled at the turn of an autumn sky.
What could I do but yell *vivas*
To baseball, milkshakes, and those sociologists
Who would clock me
As I jog into the next century
On the power of a great, silly grin.

HITCHHIKING WITH A FRIEND AND A BOOK THAT EXPLAINS THE PACIFIC OCEAN

On 41, outside Stratford,
The sky lengthens magically
When you're nineteen, the first time
On the road – and if you're
With a friend, the birds lift
And never come down in the same place.
I found myself out there, with Samuel,
Hungry as a fire, kicking rocks,

Under clouds giving up
Just as we came to believe in beauty.
It was that word, and others,
That had us pointing
To windmills and sullen cows,
The trees irresponsible with their shadows.
And it was the eagerness of grass
Under wind, a tumbleweed
Moving, a paper bag moving,
And our minds clear as water
Pooled on roadsides. We went
On for hours. The gravel
Turned under our march,
Until the landscape meant less,
And we grew tired. A banged
Truck stopped for us
And the driver's giddy dog licked
And nuzzled our necks
All through the foothills, toward Pismo Beach.
Two hours, two beers, and the sky
Hazed with mist. When we saw
A rough cut of sea through trees,
We tilted our heads, nudged each
Other's ribs, at the blue
Of waves that would end at our feet.

WALKING WITH JACKIE, SITTING WITH A DOG

Jackie on the porch, shouting for me to come out.
It's Saturday, and I am in a sweater that's
Too large, balled at the elbows, black at the collar.
Laughing, we slam the screen door on a strained
Voice, and run down the street, sticks
In hand, shooing pigeons and the girls
Who are all legs.

We cross the gray traffic
Of Belmont, and enter an alley, its quick stream
Of glass blinking in the angled light. We blink,
And throw rocks at things that move,
Slow cat or bough. We grin
Like shovels, and continue on
Because it's Saturday, early as it's ever
Going to get, and we're brothers
To all that's heaved over fences.
Our talk is nonsense: Africa and trees splintered
Into matchsticks, handlebars and the widening targets
Of his sister's breasts, staring us down.
The scattered newspaper, cartwheeling across
A street, is one way to go.
                              And we go into
Another alley, where we find a man, asleep behind
Stacked cardboard. The sun flares
Behind trees and it means little.
We find a dog, hungry and sad as a suitcase kicked open
And showing nothing. At a curb we drape
Him across our laps and quarter an orange –
The juice runs like the tears an onion would give,
If only it opened its eye.
We lick our fingers and realize
That with oranges now and plums four months away,
No one need die.

CHUY

By telephone,
By rumor,
By the shoe
That grinned ratlike
All the way
To death, Chuy

Called through
A rolled newspaper
Beyond the thin
Scaffolds of trees
Until the trees
Dropped pocked fruit
And the toppled crowns
Of bird nests.
He spoke into a cup
Of dimes, into
A paper bag
That made lunch
Of his voice,
But no answer.
It wasn't until
The eclipse
Of his sad eye
And hunger
For the forgiveness
Of trees
That the stars
Tilted earthward
And his voice
Reached, saying
He was blessed
In the name
Of a violin,
A curled shoe,
The wide stare
Of his buttonhole
That watched
His hands lock
Into a fight
Over the first
Touch of breast.

•

That night his pants
Crossed their legs
And a cockroach felt
What was dropped
From the loose
Tongues of pockets.
It meant the next day
He would sit,
Spoon in hand,
Striking the ants
That unraveled
From spools of dark
Holes. He laughed
When they were
A stain spreading
Into shadows
Trees threw out
Like seed.
He laughed and went
Inside, where
His dog
Was a suitcase of fur
Against the wall,
And the shine
Of a woman's hip
Was a frontier
He crossed before sleep.

•

The next morning
Chuy went on all
Fours, sweeping ants
Into an envelope
He licked and filed
In a coffee can;
He washed

The front window
Where December
Pressed its gray
Face, and blinked
A sadness of rain;
He hooked
A collection of stolen
Hubcaps on the wall
That separated
One dream from another —
Anything to work
Up his appetite
For the apple
That weighed
In his pocket
And kept him from
Floating face-down
Above trees
And the muted houses
Of the poor,
A knot of neighbors
Who pointed from their yards
And grew faint
As a bruise,
While Chuy drifted
And thought, "I knew
It was like this."

•

Chuy fell
For the girl
On a can of peas;
He believed
She was Norwegian
And was back
From the wheat fields,

Her skirt over
A chair, her shoes
On the windowsill
Like lamps.
He saw her reading
By this light
A tale as deep
As the woods
Of the knights
Who failed
To deepen a wound
In Grendel.
They washed
Their hands in dirt
Or spit, strained,
And returned
To a small fire
Where they pinched
Lice from each
Other's beards.
But a poor
Squire, his face a loose sack,
His wrists
Shackled in sores,
Offered a pocketknife
And asked what
Needed to be cut –
As Chuy popped a pea
Into his mouth.

•

"What about electricity,"
Chuy mused,
Unscrewing a flashlight,
Weighing the batteries
Against the hard

Light of noon.
He thumbed on
A transistor,
A fan that leafed
Through an open Bible,
And the porchlight
Hazed with an orbit
Of gnats. He
Pulled at the ends
Of his mustache,
And sat staring
At the sunlight
That lengthened
Bannerlike
Across the floor.
"Light bends,"
Chuy discovered,
Witnessing the banner
Lift onto the wall
And wave like heat.
Smiling, he washed
His hands, flylike,
And wrote in
His journal, *Light*
Is only so strong.
Closing his pen,
Chuy wondered what
He could do after lunch.

•

After lunch
Chuy lay in bed
Thinking about Virginia
And how she danced
That night —
She was a stalk

Of wheat nodding
From the lower lip
Of a farmer;
He was the one
Who leaned on a shoulder
Of cigarette smoke,
Coughing into a paper cup.
When he looked up,
Something fell
From his mouth,
And she turned away.
Later, when
She danced
The *Lava-Bed-Run,*
He blew her a kiss
And crushed a cigarette
In his palm.
Unimpressed, she moved
Into a crowd.
But near the bar,
He said, "The night
Is young, and so are you,"
Slicking back his hair
In the long waves
A sea would envy.
They strolled
To the dance floor
Where he introduced
The *Chuy-Hip-Chug,*
Shoes slipping from under
A rug of beer suds,
Arms waving
Like someone
A mile from shore
And growing breathless.

•

Chuy was downtown
At a cafe, his
Mind on toast or pie.
It was morning
And overdressed
Merchants leaned
Over cup and saucer,
Their words feeding
On the sourness
That brimmed this town.
Chuy noted
On a napkin
— a street is only so long —
And stared outside
Where already the day
Had a dog drop
Limp as a dishtowel
And the old staggering
On a crutch
Of fierce heat.
"There is meaning
In that bus, those kids,"
He thought,
And turned the dime
In his coat pocket,
Felt something
Work under his nails.
He noted on the inside
Of a matchbook cover
— it takes a coin
To ride a bus —
Paid, and entered
The street
Where he walked
A few brave steps
And propped a crutch
Under his arm.

·

Armed with an equator
Of fat, shined
Shoes, and a bad
Check, Chuy sat in
The waiting room,
His mouth dry
As a sock,
Thinking he was all right,
That the doctor
Would press here
And there, open
His mouth and offer
Him a toothbrush
And a glass of water.
The doctor would
Tap his knee,
Blow light into
His ear, and "umm"
At the milky way
Of moles on his back.
But no! The nurse
Called, told him
To undress, and it was
The doctor's cue
To say, "Looks serious,
My friend, down there."
The doctor glinting
With a needle,
Chuy backed off,
Particularly frightened
Of the cotton ball,
To the window
Where a line of sparrows
Jumped up and down
Like pistons

Which keep the day moving,
Even in a tough time like this.

•

Wherever his flashlight
Poked at night,
In the gutter
Or sloped weeds
Of his yard,
Chuy noted
Things that made
Him stroke his chin
And ask why
He was there,
Under a loose hood
Of stars, believing
That the moon's stillness
Was a lozenge
Sucked before sleep.
He bottled
A leaf, a shaving
Of bark, linked
Worms, and a trumpet
Of snail; he
Snipped a thread
From his lapel
And a lock of hair –
Gifts he buried
In a bottle
Scribbled with his name
So when the sun
Is a monocle
Pocked gray
And earth is lost
To shadow, an explorer
Far from the stars
Would know where he steps

Stepped Chuy, stooping
Among the ruins.

THERE

A yard, the pinned wash
White in the wind
Rattle of bees in a shoe box ...

I'm looking again
For a brother, his voice over my
Shoulder, behind a shed or the blue caravan of bushes –
Looking for the rain that ends beautifully
In the trees.

Where I played
There are the filth of bottles, gutted mattresses,
A dead cat on its rack of weeds.
My shadow crosses over this heap –
A broken net of flies
Lifts and comes down in knots.
Where my brother squatted over rocks,
The shattered glass and plates
From another year,
A tumbleweed and its raffle of snagged papers.

I sift the glass through my hands
And wheel the tumbleweed into a small fire.
I toss wood chips at pigeons,
Their sounds like a moment faintly remembered.

Toward dusk, toward memory,
The sun banks, silver against the junkyard.
I have much to show –
Bent nails and a pair of pliers.
This coffee-can, pressed to my ear,

Is a way to the sea ...
Wind in the china tree, and it's just over there.

HER

First I forgot your voice, then the photo you gave me.
When a leaf fell I no longer
Thought of you, shy and wordless, in a raked yard.
I no longer saw you as
The dark girl among trees,
At the entrance to a story for which
The end was always marriage and a bright car.
Your voice never came back; at night
I was left to my nonsense and a typewriter
That couldn't get things right.

This spring, ten years after, we cross
The bay to North Beach
And a bar where we grow sullen with beer.
When I say *remember*
Your eyes reflect, give back
An eagerness that makes me stare into another drink.
Looking up, I take your hand
And it's little more than a warm glove.
I take it, trying to say what it meant, at seventeen,
To lean you in a corner in East Hall
And touch between buttons
As you shivered like a machine, fearful
That someone would see us.

Tonight, no one cares,
And I fail with the light, in reaching.
Drunk, we pay with quarters
And pay again under a wheel of neon.
You hug me like a suitcase

And then send me walking
Slowly back, down a side street,
To a ticketed car and the inevitable "spare change."
On a balcony, a girl
Is singing to the banging of spoons.

THE WIDOW PEREZ

After a while
She slumped down in the closet
Among a pile of dirty clothes
To become those creases,
Gray with the meaning
Of wind, black
With the crossing of roads.
For hours she stood
In that musk, between
The slouched shoulders of shirts,
Waiting for you to return,
Your eyes the blurred points
Of twilight, your smile blank
Where a tooth was missing
And lodged with a residue
Of years.

                    But you failed
To come back, old man.
She didn't feel her warmth double
Or tug a sleeve limp
From wear; she didn't touch
Your collar flagged
And gray with distance, your mouth
Sinking into a cup
From which roots lengthen
And push upward

To what the dead say
In a sad flower ...
Hours later she came out,
Washed, and set the stove blazing.
One bowl or two? The floor ticked
And she turned to listen.

FRANKIE

Frankie Torres
Corners me
In the lunchroom,
Throws a milk
Carton at my face,
And offers a bite
Of his sandwich,
Fat with the meat
Of sad momma,
Breastless and drunk,
And hanged brother
Cut down
From the rafters
With a grape knife.
It's sour
But I swallow
Fearing the ratchet-
Wind of his fists,
The arc of spit
With girls looking on ...
We walk out
To the playground;
He wants to be
Friends, shoving me
Against a tree,
Into a pile of leaves.
Lifting me up

We stand so close
His breathing
Is familiar –
Old coat, soiled bedsheet.
He tells me
About sister howling
In a locked closet,
About his dog
Slammed against a tree
By a laughing father.
He leads me
Like a leashed dog
Past the gym
Along the chain-
Link fence, steps
Closer to Spring
When he'll drop
A neighbor
With a two-by-four,
And I'll drop my sandwich
Meatless and cold.

BULOSAN, 1935

By train
You rocked past the small towns
Where you might have married
White and worked Mexican,

Or become lost in the Chinatowns
In yellow, the tongue,
The brow, and the cocked finger –
Yellow and Filipino
Shuffle, the *carabao* walk,
The great arc of urine
Streaming in the cold.

Instead, it was L.A.
A hard cough, and blood on a shirt sleeve,
Pillow, and bedsheet
In a room narrow with sunlight.

At the table,
Your eyes two cinders in a fire,
You wrote, but nothing stopped
The black loaf of lung, the axe
Handle crossed hard over your brother.
You wrote
America is somewhere —
Now touch my hand

Until you dreamed you were a bundle
Of rags slouching
In a doorway,
A bundle poked by a cane and lifted
To a new land.
Bulosan, America slips seaward,
Swallows angle south out of reach,
And we step homeward to find
Our lives blue before TV,
Reddened with drink.

Tonight I think of that boxcar
That tunneled south
And you on blackened knuckles and bad knees.

With a finger you were mapping the ox
In the arced horizon, those stars
Drifting west to your country
When nothing could be darker
Than its pull from you.

FROM

BLACK HAIR

At eight I was brilliant with my body.
In July, that ring of heat
We all jumped through, I sat in the bleachers
Of Romain Playground, in the lengthening
Shade that rose from our dirty feet.
The game before us was more than baseball.
It was a figure – Hector Moreno
Quick and hard with turned muscles,
His crouch the one I assumed before an altar
Of worn baseball cards, in my room.

I came here because I was Mexican, a stick
Of brown light in love with those
Who could do it – the triple and hard slide,
The gloves eating balls into double plays.
What could I do with fifty pounds, my shyness,
My black torch of hair, about to go out?
Father was dead, his face no longer
Hanging over the table or our sleep,
And mother was the terror of mouths
Twisting hurt by butter knives.

In the bleachers I was brilliant with my body,
Waving players in and stomping my feet,
Growing sweaty in the presence of white shirts.
I chewed sunflower seeds. I drank water
And bit my arm through the late innings.
When Hector lined balls into deep
Center, in my mind I rounded the bases
With him, my face flared, my hair lifting
Beautifully, because we were coming home
To the arms of brown people.

I've climbed in trees
To eat, and climbed
Down to look about
This world, mouth red
From plums that were
Once clouds in March
– rain I mean, that
Pitiless noise against
Leaves and branches.
Father once lifted me
Into one, and from
A distance I might
Have been a limb,
Moving a little heavier
Than most but a limb
All the same. My hands
Opened like mouths,
The juice running
Without course down
My arms, as I stabbed
For plums, bunched
Or half-hidden behind
Leaves. A bird fluttered
From there, a single
Leaf cutting loose,
And gnats like smoke
Around a bruised plum.
I climbed searching
For those red globes,
And with a sack filled,
I called for father
To catch – father
Who would disappear
Like fruit at the end
Of summer, from a neck

Wound some say — blood
Running like the juice
Of these arms. I
Twisted the throat
Of the sack, tossed
It, and started down
To father, his mouth
Already red and grinning
Like the dead on their
Rack of blackness.
When I jumped, he was
Calling, arms open,
The sack at his feet
For us, the half-bitten,
Who bring on the flies.

ORANGES

The first time I walked
With a girl, I was twelve,
Cold, and weighted down
With two oranges in my jacket.
December. Frost cracking
Beneath my steps, my breath
Before me, then gone,
As I walked toward
Her house, the one whose
Porch light burned yellow
Night and day, in any weather.
A dog barked at me, until
She came out pulling
At her gloves, face bright
With rouge. I smiled,
Touched her shoulder, and led
Her down the street, across

A used car lot and a line
Of newly planted trees,
Until we were breathing
Before a drugstore. We
Entered, the tiny bell
Bringing a saleslady
Down a narrow aisle of goods.
I turned to the candies
Tiered like bleachers,
And asked what she wanted —
Light in her eyes, a smile
Starting at the corners
Of her mouth. I fingered
A nickel in my pocket,
And when she lifted a chocolate
That cost a dime,
I didn't say anything.
I took the nickel from
My pocket, then an orange,
And set them quietly on
The counter. When I looked up,
The lady's eyes met mine,
And held them, knowing
Very well what it was all
About.

      Outside,
A few cars hissing past,
Fog hanging like old
Coats between the trees.
I took my girl's hand
In mine for two blocks,
Then released it to let
Her unwrap the chocolate.
I peeled my orange
That was so bright against
The gray of December

That, from some distance,
Someone might have thought
I was making a fire in my hands.

BEHIND GRANDMA'S HOUSE

At ten I wanted fame. I had a comb
And two Coke bottles, a tube of Bryl-creem.
I borrowed a dog, one with
Mismatched eyes and a happy tongue,
And wanted to prove I was tough
In the alley, kicking over trash cans,
A dull chime of tuna cans falling.
I hurled light bulbs like grenades
And men teachers held their heads,
Fingers of blood lengthening
On the ground. I flicked rocks at cats,
Their goofy faces spurred with foxtails.
I kicked fences. I shooed pigeons.
I broke a branch from a flowering peach
And frightened ants with a stream of spit.
I said "*Chale*," "In your face," and "No way
Daddy-O" to an imaginary priest
Until grandma came into the alley,
Her apron flapping in a breeze,
Her hair mussed, and said, "Let me help you,"
And punched me between the eyes.

BROWN GIRL, BLONDE OKIE
for Scott Bartlett

Jackie and I cross-legged
In the yard, plucking at
Grass, cupping flies

And shattering them against
Each other's faces –
Smiling that it's summer,
No school, and we can
Sleep out under stars
And the blink of jets
Crossing up our lives.
The flies leave, or die,
And we are in the dark,
Still cross-legged,
Talking not dogs or baseball,
But whom will we love,
What brown girl or blonde
Okie to open up to
And say we are sorry
For our faces, the filth
We shake from our hair,
The teeth without direction.
"We're ugly," says Jackie
On one elbow, and stares
Lost between jets
At what this might mean.
In the dark I touch my
Nose, trace my lips, and pinch
My mouth into a dull flower.
Oh God, we're in trouble.

HEAVEN

Scott and I bent
To the radio, legs
Twitching to The Stones,
Faces wet, arms rising
And falling as if
Trying to get out or
Crawl the air – the

Air thick with our
Toweled smells.

                          It's
'64, and our room
And its shaft of dust,
Turning, is all
There is – though Mamma
Says there's the car
To wash, the weeds,
The grass, and garbage
Tilting on the back steps.
"Yeh, yeh," we scream
Behind the closed door,
And boost the radio
To "10" and begin
Bouncing on the bed,
Singing, making up
Words about this girl,
That car, tears,
Lipstick, handjives
In alleys – bouncing
Hard, legs split, arms
Open for the Lord,
Until Scott can't stand it
And crashes through
The screened window
And tumbles into a bush,
His shoulders locked
Between branches,
His forehead scratched,
But still singing,
"Baby, baby, o baby."

LEARNING TO BARGAIN

Summer. Flies knitting
Filth on the window,
A mother calling a son home ...
I'm at that window, looking
Onto the street: dusk,
A neighbor kid sharpening
A stick at the curb.
I go outside and sit
Next to him without saying
A word. When he looks
Up, his eyes dark as flies ...
I ask about the cat, the one dead
Among weeds in the alley.
"Yeah, I did it," he admits,
And stares down at his feet,
Then my feet. "What do you want?"
"A dime," I say. Without
Looking at me, he gets
Up, goes behind his house,
And returns with two Coke bottles.
"These make a dime." He sits
At the curb, his shoulders
So bony they could be wings
To lift him so far. "Don't tell."
He snaps a candy into halves
And we eat in silence.

ODE TO THE YARD SALE

A toaster,
A plate
Of pennies,
A plastic rose

Staring up
To the sky.
It's Saturday
And two friends,
Merchants of
The salvageable heart,
Are throwing
Things onto
The front lawn –
A couch,
A beanbag,
A table to clip
Poodles on,
Drawers of
Potato mashers,
Spoons, knives
That signaled
To the moon
For help.
Rent is due.
It's somewhere
On this lawn,
Somewhere among
The shirts we've
Looked good in,
Taken off before
We snuggled up
To breasts
That almost made
Us gods.
It'll be a good
Day, because
There's much
To sell,
And the pitcher
Of water
Blue in the shade,

Clear in the
Light, with
The much-handled
Scotch the color
Of leaves
Falling at our
Shoes, will
Get us through
The afternoon
Rush of old
Ladies, young women
On their way
To becoming nurses,
Bachelors of
The twice-dipped
Tea bag. It's
An eager day:
Wind in the trees,
Laughter of
Children behind
Fences. Surely
People will arrive
With handbags
And wallets,
To open up coffee
Pots and look
In, weigh pans
In each hand,
And prop hats
On their heads
And ask, "How do
I look?" (foolish
To most,
Beautiful to us).
And so they
Come, poking
At the clothes,

Lifting salt
And pepper shakers
For their tiny music,
Thumbing through
Old magazines
For someone
They know,
As we sit with
Our drinks
And grow sad
That the ashtray
Has been sold,
A lamp, a pillow,
The fry pans
That were action
Packed when
We cooked,
Those things
We threw so much
Love on, day
After day,
Sure they would
Mean something
When it came
To this.

AMBITION

For years our ambition was to eat
Chicken. To sit in a back yard,
In an aftershock of heat
When the sun was out of the way.
This happened. Drunk under a tree
We became sophisticates of the lawn chair
And beer bottles – trumpets we raised

All night under those bitter stars
That turned us to our lies
Of women, lost and found door to door.
"I was lonely once," I told them
And they booed and flicked beer tops
At me – told me to get into
The kitchen for the hard stuff.
When I returned, Chris the failed
Scholar of three degrees
Talked Italy. Flames broke
From the hibachi. The chicken
Grew noisy as a Latin mob.
"Quiet," Jon yelled, and poked them
With a fork onto the platter.
We went inside to argue over salad
– a gaudy hat we stuffed into our mouths –
And let food climb our elbows.
Dogs snapped at bones, whined, jumped
When we threw them buttered rolls,
Corn, rings of potato. We ate
Like Romans with good jobs
And returned to the back yard
To find that the moon had moved
Our chairs. Lost them in fact.
We dropped on the grass, on elbows.
The moon was clearing the trees
By two fingers. I took bets
We'd be happy. "No one ever knows,"
The scholar sighed, empty trumpet
In hand. I smiled. Jon smiled.
Cats with full lives grinned
From the back fence. Sniffed.
Dropped to the ground to nudge us for
The love of chicken but love all the same.

THE ESTONIAN COMES TO DINNER
for Jon Veinberg

Again I dream the frying pan
Is endless, the tomatoes fat,
The cheese blunt as women on barstools.
I am yours. I take you
To my mouth, the suggestive
Radish at hand, the celery
Clutched like a microphone.
I speak, and important people take note.
I say there's nothing more,
This plate and abused napkin, that wine
Whose memory is deeper than mine.
Estonian, let's show off tonight,
And suck these bones dry, into
Fine slivers that will give off light.
When we eat, let panic rule.
Let cop cars circle the block
And dogs turn on their leashes, crying.
Far off, in the countryside,
Let the cows go to their knees
And hens flutter like books
Thrown from speeding cars.
But we're not going anywhere.
The table is here. The pear that
Was once rain is at hand.
The bread is at hand – the butter,
The potato baked twice
And poked with many eyes.
Let the day end and us begin,
The fork, the knife, the plate all useless.

KEARNEY PARK

True Mexicans or not, let's open our shirts
And dance, a spark of heels
Chipping at the dusty cement. The people
Are shiny like the sea, turning
To the clockwork of *rancheras,*
The accordion wheezing, the drum-tap
Of work rising and falling.
Let's dance with our hats in hand.
The sun is behind the trees,
Behind my stutter of awkward steps
With a woman who is a brilliant arc of smiles,
An armful of falling water. Her skirt
Opens and closes. My arms
Know no better but to flop
On their own, and we spin, dip,
And laugh into each other's faces –
Faces that could be famous
On the coffee table of my *abuelita.*
But grandma is here, at the park, with a beer
At her feet, clapping
And shouting, "Dance, hijo, dance!"
Laughing, I bend, slide, and throw up
A great cloud of dust,
Until the girl and I are no more.

MORNING ON THIS STREET

It's Saturday with the gray
Noise of rain at the window,
Its fingers weeping to get in.
We're in bunk beds, one brother
Talking football, another
Turning to the dreamed girl

He'd jump from a tree to die for.
Later, in the kitchen,
He tells me, Love is like snow
Or something. I listen
With a bowl at the stove, dress,
And go outside to trees dripping
Rain, a pickup idling
With its headlights on.
I look for something to do
Slowly with a stick
In the absence of love,
That Catholic skirt in a pew.
I walk banging fences
Until Earl the Cartman rattles
Onto our block – a rope over
His shoulder. He pulls hard
Because his wife, centered
On that cart, is cold
Under the rough temple
Of cardboard he's cut for her.
Her legs are bundled in strips
Of white cloth, half there
With the dead, half with us
Who have oranges to give,
As he steps heavily toward
The trees they'll call
Home – a small fire and the black
Haunt of smoke. It's for his wife
That he lives and pulls a rope
To its frayed end. The sky
Is nothing and these neighbors
Wincing behind windows
Are even less. This is marriage,
A man and a woman, in one kind of weather.

At a city square
Children laugh in the red
Sweaters of Catholics,
As they walk home between trucks
And sunlight angled off buildings that end in points.
I'm holding an apple, among shoppers
Clutching bags big enough to sleep in,
And the air is warm for October –
Torn pieces of paper
Scuttling like roaches, a burst at a time.

The children are blond,
Shiny, and careful at the lights –
The sister with her brother's hand.
They cross looking
At their watches, and I cross too.
I want to know where
They're going, what door they'll push
Open and call home –
The TV coming on,
Milk, a cookie for each hand.

As a kid I wanted to live
In the city, in a building that rose above it all,
The gray streets burst open, a rattle
Of jackhammers. I wanted to
Stare down from the eighteenth floor, and let things go –
My homework for one, a paper plane
With a half-drawn heart and a girl's name.
I wanted to say that I ate
And slept, ate and slept in a building
That faced other buildings, a sliver of sea
Blue in the distance.
I wanted to hear voices
Behind walls, the *click-click* of a poodle

Strolling to his bowl – a violin like fingers
Running down a blackboard.
I wanted to warm my hands at a teakettle
And comb my hair in an elevator, my mouth
Still rolling with cereal, as I started off
For school, a row of pens in my shirt pocket.
Back home at the window
I wanted it to be December –
Flags and honking cars,
A Santa Claus with his pot, a single red
Balloon let go and racing skyward,
And the tiny mothers who would come around
Buildings, disappear, and come around again,
Hugging bags for all they were worth to children.

FAILING IN THE PRESENCE OF ANTS

We live to some purpose, daughter.
Across the park, among
The trees that give the eye
Something to do, let's spread
A blanket on the ground
And examine the ants, loose
Thread to an old coat.
Perhaps they are more human than we are.
They live for the female,
Rescue their hurt, and fall earthward
For their small cause. And
Us? We live for our bellies,
The big O of our mouths.
Give me, give me, they say,
And many people, whole countries,
May go under because we desire TV
And chilled drinks, clothes
That hang well on our bodies –

Desire sofas and angled lamps,
Hair the sea may envy
On a slow day.
It is hurtful to sweep
Ants into a frenzy, blow
Chemicals into their eyes –
Those austere marchers who will lift
Their heads to rumor – seed,
Wafer of leaf, dropped apple –
And start off, over this
And that, between sloppy feet
And staggered chairs, for no
Purpose other than it might be good.

SHOPPING FOR A WOMAN

Shopping for my wife, I'm lost
To the shrug of skirts, taut calves,
The hair coming up with the wind – these women
With their arms hurting for one more red gift.
OK, I admit it. I'm the Catholic
In the lingerie department
Tapping slippers against my palm
And weighing nighties that are sheer as clouds,
Upfront and eager to crumble in my hands.
I buy the cloud, and on the next floor,
A woman behind a counter with
Patou, Givenchy, L'Aire du Temps
Under my nose, splashed on my wrist.
Her throat is open, eyes arched like birds,
And the dark behind her ear is a channel
To the heart. I ask, Is this what women
Want? She lifts her eyes to me
And the birds are gone: her face is fawn-colored,
Quiet in her study of me. Sometimes,

She says, and looks aside to a tray
Of jewelry – pearl necklace,
Earrings showing light. These things too,
She says. And this chain, in gold.

SATURDAY UNDER THE SKY

This morning, with the rain tapping
The shoulders of everyone we will ever love –
Your mother for one, those dogs
Trotting for leaves –
We could go to the aquarium –
Angel fish and eels, the gray plop
Of toads among rocks. We
Could walk slowly, with a balloon
Banging against my head,
Walk with other fathers and
Daughters tapping the glass cases
For the lizard to waken
And the snake roll from
One dried limb to the next. We
Could handle a starfish, lift
A spiny thing, green in the water,
Blue in our hands. Instead
It's the Hall of Science
Where we stand before mirrors
That stretch us tall, then squeeze us
Squat as suitcases bound for Chicago.
There are rocks, the strata
Of earth, a black cut of oil far down.
There are computers, a maze of lights
And wires, steel balls bouncing
About – they could be us, if we should make
The moon one day. But you tire
In a room mixed up with stars

And it's juice and a pretzel
On the bench, with me thinking
I'm a good father. When we leave
Rain is still tapping shoulders
With everyone looking around,
Hunched in their coats.
The wind picks at the trees,
At the shrubs. The sky rolls and
The balloon tied to your wrist is banging
Unfairly against my head: *What else! What else!*

FINDING A LUCKY NUMBER

When I was like you I crossed a street
To a store, and from the store
Up an alley, as I rolled chocolate
In my mouth and looked around
With my face. The day was blue
Between trees, even without wind,
And the fences were steaming
And a dog was staring into a paint bucket
And a Mexicano was raking
Spilled garbage into a box,
A raffle of eggshells and orange peels.
He nodded his head and I nodded mine
And rolled chocolate all the way
To the courthouse, where I sat
In the park, with a leaf falling
For every person who passed –
Three leaves and three daughters
With bags in their hands.
I followed them under trees,
The leaves rocking out of reach
Like those skirts I would love
From a distance. I lost them

When I bent down to tie my shoes
And begged a squirrel to eat grass.
Looking up, a dog on the run,
A grandma with a cart,
And Italians clicking dominoes
At a picnic table – men
Of the old world, in suits big enough
For Europe. I approached
Them like a squirrel, a tree
At a time, and when I was close
Enough to tell the hour from their wrists,
One laughed with hands in his hair
And turned to ask my age.
"Twelve," I said, and he knocked
My head softly with a knuckle:
"Lucky number, Sonny." He bared
His teeth, yellow and crooked
As dominoes, and tapped the front ones
With a finger. "I got twelve – see."
He opened wide until his eyes were lost
In the pouches of fat cheeks,
And I, not knowing what to do, looked in.

LOOKING AROUND, BELIEVING

How strange that we can begin at any time.
With two feet we get down the street.
With a hand we undo the rose.
With an eye we lift up the peach tree
And hold it up to the wind – white blossoms
At our feet. Like today. I started
In the yard with my daughter,
With my wife poking at a potted geranium,
And now I am walking down the street,
Amazed that the sun is only so high,

Just over the roof, and a child
Is singing through a rolled newspaper
And a terrier is leaping like a flea
And at the bakery I pass, a palm,
Like a suctioning starfish, is pressed
To the window. We're keeping busy –
This way, that way, we're making shadows
Where sunlight was, making words
Where there was only noise in the trees.

THE TREES THAT CHANGE OUR LIVES

When I was twenty I walked past
The lady I would marry –
Cross-legged on the porch.
She was cracking walnuts
With a hammer, a jar
At her side. I had come
From the store, swinging
A carton of cold beers,
And when I looked she smiled.
And that was all, until
I came back, flushed,
Glowing like a lantern
Against a backdrop
Of silly one-liners –
Cute-face, peaches, baby-lips.

We talked rain, cats,
About rain on cats,
And later went inside
For a sandwich, a glass
Of milk, sweets.
Still later, a month later,
We were going at one

Another on the couch, bed,
In the bathtub
And its backwash of bubbles,
Snapping. So it went,
And how strangely: the walnut
Tree had dropped its hard
Fruit, and they, in turn,
Were dropped into a paper
Bag, a jar, then into
The dough that was twisted
Into bread for the love
Of my mouth, so
It might keep talking.

BETWEEN WORDS

Just what is there to do? Eat
Is one, sleep is another.
But before the night ends
We could walk under
These camphors, hand in hand
If you like, namedropping
The great cities of the past,
And if a dog should join
Us with his happy tail,
The three of us could talk,
Politics perhaps, medicine
If our feet should hurt
For the sea.

      Love,
The moon is between clouds,
And we're between words
That could deepen
But never arrive.

Like this walk. We could go
Under trees and moons,
With the stars tearing
Like mouths in the night sky,
And we'll never arrive.
That's the point. To go
Hand in hand, with the words
A sparrow could bicker
Over, a dog could make sense of
Even behind a closed door,
Is what it's about.
A friend says, be happy. Desire.
Remember the blossoms
In rain, because in the end
Not even the ants
Will care who we were
When they climb our faces
To undo the smiles.

FROM

WHO WILL KNOW US?

A RED PALM

You're in this dream of cotton plants.
You raise a hoe, swing, and the first weeds
Fall with a sigh. You take another step,
Chop, and the sigh comes again,
Until you yourself are breathing that way
With each step, a sigh that will follow you into town.

That's hours later. The sun is a red blister
Coming up in your palm. Your back is strong,
Young, not yet the broken chair
In an abandoned school of dry spiders.
Dust settles on your forehead, dirt
Smiles under each fingernail.
You chop, step, and by the end of the first row,
You can buy one splendid fish for wife
And three sons. Another row, another fish,
Until you have enough and move on to milk,
Bread, meat. Ten hours and the cupboards creak.
You can rest in the back yard under a tree.
Your hands twitch on your lap,
Not unlike the fish on a pier or the bottom
Of a boat. You drink iced tea. The minutes jerk
Like flies.

It's dusk, now night,
And the lights in your home are on.
That costs money, yellow light
In the kitchen. That's thirty steps,
You say to your hands,
Now shaped into binoculars.
You could raise them to your eyes:
You were a fool in school, now look at you.
You're a giant among cotton plants.
Now you see your oldest boy, also running.
Papa, he says, it's time to come in.

You pull him into your lap
And ask, What's forty times nine?
He knows as well as you, and you smile.
The wind makes peace with the trees,
The stars strike themselves in the dark.
You get up and walk with the sigh of cotton plants.
You go to sleep with a red sun on your palm,
The sore light you see when you first stir in bed.

ANOTHER TIME

The stars are eating through the sky
Now that it's twilight, hour
When in the back yard
I can do no more than a tree:
Bend, flutter, root myself in wind.
For me guilt keeps the flesh going.
I look around. The pond is blowing
With lines. The fuchsia, bright lantern
Of flowers, moves in the breeze,
And our cat scratches on the fence.
And what I don't see I hear:
Daughter in her room cutting paper
With toy scissors. My wife
Is in the front yard, watering.
This all stops. I give myself over
To what uncle said: that it was father,
Then dead three years, and his steps
Rounding the house to the back porch
Twice a week – crunch of gravel
And a presence at the door.
When I close my eyes, he's on the steps,
Brow of sadness, his Pendleton open
From the wind that climbs in the junkyard –
Along the alley, silhouette of iron

And pipes held against the sky.
That's how we leave. We die in
Such places. Like father,
Whom we miss and don't know,
Who would have saved us
From those terrible years
If that day at work he got up
Hurt but alive. He fell
From that ladder with an upturned palm,
With the eyes of watery light.
We went on with sorrow that found no tree
To cry from. I can't go to his grave.
I know this. I can't find my place
Or wake up and say, Let him walk,
Let him round the house but not come in.
Even the sun with so much to give must fall.

THE SEVENTIETH YEAR

We hear you want to die.
What is it?
The hair on an arm
Leaning toward the shadows?

Sun-Maid is gone, Grandpa,
The machinery fleeced in rust.
Though the loading dock holds the years
Of rain, sweat that fell
And opened into momentary coins,
Work has stopped. You can sleep now.
Sunlight enters the house,
Dust drifts in a galaxy
Of unmapped motes. And Grandma?
She is well – her veins no longer
Surfacing under a blue flesh.

She's with you now
And you smell the warmth
Of her nightly presence.
Get up and eat, Grandpa.
Your skin has yellowed.
Look at the backyard garden –
Already the flower beds
Brim with summer weeds
And ants unravel
From their dark holes in the trees.
Come to the kitchen.
It is warm there, Grandpa,
And your family, the little ones
With their cards of Get Well,
Has gathered like a small cloud,
Like the steam weeping
On the window.

HEAVEN

They say that it's not at all white,
That the freeze going up
Is momentary,

Then the full remembrance:
The alley with its morning fog,
Father, piping soup
On the stove's blue rings.
Then the *and* and *and* of a child's first years.

Maybe you sit in a chair.
Maybe earth is far below.
The string that ties you to that place
Is just a waver,
Spider skein two thousand years down.

Or maybe the new home is much closer,
Just above the trees,
A sea howl at the window
— or you're those hangers banging
Quietly when the closet door opens.

Conjectures. Little clues,
Really. But we're hopeful that we'll wake.
The chair is for us. The sorting
Of days is done on our fingers.

Lost boot, first girl,
Scar on the chin with its pink hook.

EVE

It was on your father's workbench
In the barn that you undid
Your skirt: hair, kinked hair
Thick as a child's black scribbling,
Pink when you breathed
And opened. You watched
Me watch you. The barn ticked.
Pigeons shifted in the rafters,
Their wings like prayers as we made
Hurt noises and blood cried from
A new wound. Scared, you left,
And I counted to a hundred
Before I walked out. Shame
Rode on my shoes with the dust.
I looked up. Your father,
A good man, was on the ditch bank,
Irrigating. I drank water
From the hose, watched you watch me.
You climbed back up the fruit ladder
With a peach bucket on your hip.

I was a boy. I hurried home, scared
By then, because the bucket
Was a baby nine months
From that morning when we said
"Let's try," and pulled at each other,
The bench chirping from a loose bolt,
Or was it love and that bolt?
How we thought we knew. Big friends
Said it should hurt the first time,
Then stop, that we would become
Man and woman, and drive long cars,
– life like a pinwheel in the air.
Eve, country girl with babies
Like melons, with no daddy
For the crying – how they lied.

ELEGY
for Sadao Oda

The mountain, snow-covered in April,
And the bushes at our feet, along the cliffs,
Firing into tiger-orange blossoms.
Early morning and we drive toward Sequoia,
To get away from the house, the dead hours
And sadness, black branch of sparrows just out the window.
We went by Belmont, past Minkler and Old Town,
And tried to be happy not once but twice –
Bought apples from a farmer with root-cold hands,
Watched sheep, fat as couches, on a green roll of hill.
When we called, they turned the other way.
When we slammed the car door, they looked back,
Their eyes of wet stone.

At a toppled roadside stand, five thousand
Feet above the valley, the haze
Is feather-colored, far away

Like you who are no longer with us,
You who in your time thinned grapes,
Hoed beets, stood muddy in boots,
The waters of twilight filling the rows of cotton.
Work. Work and fish is what you did.
Saintly in the shine of your work-polished clothes
You skinned the persimmon with an ancient knife,
Assuring your granddaughter, "This is good. You'll see."
In this air, thin-blue, we don't say much.
Wind plays in our hair. A bee circles lazily
The sweetness of a crushed can.
Not yet noon, and already we're losing the day.

LOOKING FOR A CEMETERY

We drove looking for that place,
Academy Cemetery, and found broken asphalt,
Fence posts, cows with boulder-sized heads
Hanging over barbed wire, drooling.
We looked at one another and turned off the radio.
It seemed that we were lost, and we slowed
The car until its shadow caught up. Brown grass
Glittered bottles and the cellophane
Wrappers of cigarette packs, flattened cans,
Pie tins, and sheet metal. We pulled to the side,
Got out, and walked with hands in our pockets,
Both of us loving the sound
Of gravel under foot. It was Saturday
In Fresno, but in the foothills, a quiet Sunday.
We walked without saying much,
A nod at a bird, a tap on the shoulder
When rabbits sprang across the road.
The cemetery was close by we knew,
Over that ridge, behind the rise of railroad track.
The dead can't get up and just go,

We thought, and stood in the sun,
Cheated by our dollar map.
                              But when the wind picked up,
When a leaf sparkled we guessed the three oak trees.
When we started over, running uphill,
The grass grew tall enough to whisper at our thighs.

WHO WILL KNOW US?
for Jaroslav Seifert

It is cold, bitter as a penny.
I'm on a train, rocking toward the cemetery
To visit the dead who now
Breathe through the grass, through me,
Through relatives who will come
And ask, Where are you?
Cold. The train with its cargo
Of icy coal, the conductor
With his loose buttons like heads of crucified saints,
His mad puncher biting zeros through tickets.

The window that looks onto its slate of old snow.
Cows. The barbed fences throat-deep in white.
Farm houses dark, one wagon
With a shivering horse.
This is my country, white with no words,
House of silence, horse that won't budge
To cast a new shadow. Fence posts
That are the people, spotted cows the machinery
That feed Officials. I have nothing
Good to say. I love Paris
And write, "Long Live Paris!"
I love Athens and write,
"The great book is still in her lap."
Bats have intrigued me,

The pink vein in a lilac.
I've longed to open an umbrella
In an English rain, smoke
And not give myself away,
Drink and call a friend across the room,
Stomp my feet at the smallest joke.
But this is my country.
I walk a lot, sleep.
I eat in my room, read in my room,
And make up women in my head –
Nostalgia, the cigarette lighter from before the war,
Beauty, tears that flow inward to feed its roots.

The train. Red coal of evil.
We are its passengers, the old and young alike.
Who will know us when we breathe through the grass?

MAGNETS

I click the plastic faces of kewpie dolls
Together – they want to kiss but can't.
The magnets behind their heads have died
Out, and wouldn't pull iron filings
From the loosest dirt, let alone show
Affection, smack lips, or clunk heads
And make my bashful nephew say,
Ah, that's for sissies.

                    They stare at each other,
Shyly with hands behind their backs,
Black lash of youth, pink cheeks of first time.
But it's over for them. The magnets
Have died out. I drink my coffee
And think of old girlfriends,

How we too clunked heads together,
Kissed and clunked until that pull of love
Stopped and we just looked.

Sometimes the magnets fall from our heads,
Settle in our hips. Beds are ruined
This way. Books tumble from crowded shelves
When couples clunk waists together,
With the women looking at ceilings,
Men at loose hair on pillows,
And then it's the other way around.
But magnets die out. They grow heavy,
These stones that could sharpen knives
Or bring faces together for one last kiss.

For years I thought iron lived forever,
Certainly longer than love. Now I have doubts.
The kewpie dolls, set on starched doilies
On my grandmother's television,
Smile but don't touch. The paint is flaking,
Dust is a faint aura of loss. Grandmother loved
Her husband for five decades, and still does,
Poor grandpa who is gone. They worked
Side by side in fields, boxed raisins,
Raised children in pairs. Now grandmother
Wants to die but doesn't know how.
Her arms are frail, her eyes of cataract
Can't hold a face. *Hijo, hijo,*
She says, and looks over my shoulder.
It's blinding wisdom to see her on the edge
Of her couch. The magnet is in her feet,
Ready to gather up the earth.

When we fired our rifles
We spooked sparrows from the tree.
Bottles burst when we aimed,
Tin cans did more than *ping*
And throw themselves in dry grass.
The dog pulled in tail and ears,
Saddened his eyes and crawled under the car.
We smiled at this, Leonard and I,
And went to look at the tin cans
And push our fingers into the holes –
Pink worms wagging at our happiness.
We set them up again, blew jagged zeros
On all sides, and then sat down
To eat sandwiches, talk about girls,
School, and how to get by on five-dollar dates.
Finished eating, we called the dog
With finger snaps and tongue clicks,
But he crawled deeper into shadow.
We searched the car trunk for Coke cans,
Found three, and set them farther away.
We raised the rifles, winced an eye,
And fired, Leonard hitting
On the third try, me on the fifth.
We jumped up and down, laughed, and waved
A hand through the drifts of gun smoke,
Then the two of us returned to the car
Where we dragged the dog into the back seat.
We started the engine, let it idle in smoke,
And raised our rifles one last time,
The grass and dirt leaping into air.
We laughed and took a step back,
Packed the rifles in oily blankets,
And revved the engine. We turned onto the road
Without a good thought in our heads,
Ready for life.

The public library was saying things
In so many books,
And I, Catholic boy
In a green sweater,
Was reading the same page
A hundred times.
A girl was in my way,
Protestant or Jew,
And she was at the other end
Of the oak table,
Her hands like doves
On the encyclopedia, E-G.
England, I thought,
Germany before the war?
She'll copy from that book,
Cursive like waves
Riding to the shore,
And tomorrow walk across lawns
In a public school dress
With no guilt pulling at an ear.
And me? I'll kick
My Catholic shoes through
Leaves, stand in the
Cloakroom and eat
A friend's lunch. My work
Was never finished.
My maps were half-colored,
History a stab in the dark,
And fractions the inside
Of a pocket watch
Spilled on my desk.
I was no good. And who do I
Blame? That girl.
When she scribbled a pink
Eraser and her pony

Tails bounced like skirts,
I looked up, gazed for what
My mother and sister could not
Offer, then returned to
The same sentence: *the Nile*
Is the longest river in the world.
A pencil rolled from the
Table when she clicked open
Her binder. I looked up,
Gazed, looked back down:
The Nile is the longest river ...

LEARNING MY LESSON

When I was five I found
Beauty – a girl on a box
Of soap – while fooling in
An alley with my brother
Who was all gum and
Better looks. He snatched
The box, gazed, and
Looked back at me, kid
With spiky hair and teeth
Like a broken-down fence
– said he knew her house
And took me down our alley
To the street Mother said never
To cross. "Over there,"
He pointed, "that house."
I worried my brow into lines:
Stacked boards, oily field
Of truck parts, a warehouse
Slamming shut with
Machinery. "No sir,"
I said, being no one's fool,

And ran away to play
Only to return, look both ways,
And cross the street.
I looked back. A river
Of glass and bottle
Caps gleamed on the asphalt.
The parked cars seemed far,
Even Rick who was jumping
In delight, singing I was a dead boy
On the floor when Momma found out.
"You're stupid too," I said,
Turned and walked until
I was lost and talking
To a dog. And how did I
Get back? How did any of us
Get back when we searched
For beauty? I don't know,
Except days later
Our neighbor's cat crossed
That same street and came home
With a sliver, long as an evil finger,
Poking from its eye.
Poor orange cat, it couldn't tear,
Blink, or close its eye in sleep,
Even in death.

CONFESSION TO MRS. ROBERT L. SNOW

I can clear my name.
It was my brother, not me,
Who stole your fruit
And sold that pop
Bottle on your porch
(with our pennies we
Bought jaw breakers

That shattered like stars
When Mother got us home,
Naked with our two sins).
It was my brother, not me.
I was saintly inside and out,
And walked through puddles
In a Catholic sweater,
Even though it was
Summer and no school.
Good on Sundays,
I could jump from a chair
And spell my name three times
Before I dropped to my feet.
I jumped from the fence,
The incinerator, the house
– air all around for
Seconds and me flapping
As I spelled the holy
Countries of the world,
Yugoslavia as best I could.
My brother watched,
Sister with a Tootsie Roll
That was yet another
Bottle from your porch
Watched with fangs
Of candy in her mouth.
They witnessed me hang
In the air. They shouted
For me to fly over to the tree,
Your tree, and come back
With yellow-green apricots.
I leaped beyond the clothes
Line and found myself
In the bush, knocked with
Lumps where a halo would rest.
I touched this sparkling hurt
And ran inside to ask

Mother if there was blood.
Horns, she said
With her witch's mouth,
Devil horns! My sweater
Went limp on my body.
God gives me a mother
Like this? To hell
With the saints! I kicked
Puddles as I walked
To your house, not flew,
And let the apricots
And pop bottles alone.
While you watered
The front yard, I sneaked
Through the back door
And took a happy dollar
From your purse.
I laughed into my hands.
Horns, I whispered,
Big horns for me.

SMALL TOWN WITH ONE ROAD

We could be here. This is the valley
And its black strip of highway, big-eyed
With rabbits that won't get across.
Kids could make it, though.
They leap barefoot to the store –
Sweetness on their tongues, red stain of laughter.
A hot dime falls from their palms,
Chinks of light, and they eat
Candies all the way home
Where there's a dog for each hand,
Cats, chickens in the yard.
A pot bangs and water runs in the kitchen.

Beans, they think, and beans it will be,
Brown soup that's muscle for fieldwork
And the tired steps to a fruit ladder.
Okie or Mexican, Jew that got lost,
It's a hard life where the sun looks.
The cotton gin stands tall in the money dream
And the mill is a paycheck for the wife,
Or perhaps even my wife, who once boxed peaches
And plums, hoed Papa's field that wavered like a mirage.
We could go back. I could lose my job,
This easy one that's only words,
And pick up a shovel, hoe, broom to take it
Away. Worry is my daughter's story.
She touches my hand. We suck roadside
Snowcones in the shade and look about.
Behind sunglasses I see where I stood: brown kid
Getting across. "He's like me,"
I tell my daughter, and she stops her mouth.
He looks both ways and then leaps
Across the road where riches
Happen on a red tongue.

THE PHILOSOPHY OF DOG & MAN
for Jeff Knight

Stray dogs come with the rain,
Two hours before the garbage men
And their elephant noise of truck
Crushing eggshell and tuna can,
Light bulbs with their bleak rattle.
Or so I hear. I struggle into slippers,
Part the curtain: a tall dog,
Paws up on the heap, is
Working on a sour casserole,
The noodles marching into his mouth,

And a moist nose sniffing
For chicken bone and week-old stew,
For pie tins with buttery crust.
I've never seen happiness
Over a bone with little meat,
Happiness in rain. This
Is what I want, to be up before light,
To be in rain with garbage men.
On the back porch, I snap
A finger, call "Here boy,"
And the dog throws down its ears,
Ashamed to be caught eating.
I show him the pink emptiness of my palm,
But what am I to him? He doesn't know me.
I'm a man in a robe, not a friend
Of green alleys and poor days,
A man in slippers climbing
Pathetically down wet stairs.
Hurried love trots away on three legs,
The hurt paw touching ground
Only when he looks back.

GOOD MORNING, FRESNO

I want to stay in bed.
The heat is kicking the front door,
And our daughter, angel
In panties turned inside out,
Is chasing a fly with a toilet roll.

It's a game for her, anger for me,
That fly orbiting my head.
I pull the sheet over my face.
My wife is there,
Groaning that she doesn't want to get up.

She opens a red eye, and I close
Mine: I see the snow
Of give-away bank calendars,
Fruit, rocks hugged for their cold,
And clouds hauling in fall.

When I close my eyes
It's still there: the day
Sweating like a mule. What God
Invented summer? I need two washcloths,
A wet one to cool the body,
A dry one to hide my face
From what's coming:

The door opens.
A *clip-clop* enters the bedroom.
The mule. It hangs its head, big as a suitcase,
Over the bed. Flies whine from its ear,
Jump, make their sticky living off each toe.

AT THE ALL-NIGHT CAFE
for Omar Salinas

America is at work. There is the splotch of blue neon
Behind the left leg, renegade line in the right eye.
My favorite waitress is walking three hot plates,

The enchilada special with extra red
And a row of olives crucified by toothpicks.
She bounces from table to table,

With the lead-stink of bitterness on her tongue,
With the vinegary rag to wipe up what the Fat Boys
Let fall from their drunken forks.

The cluttered table is where the mad ate.
Their mess is her mess; her breasts shake
Their sweaty holsters as she digs fingernails

Into dried egg and scrubs. Her skirt goes up
Like a curtain when she bends for a clean spoon.
No one bothers to turn. The patrons

Stir their coffee, poke the yellow
From snotty eggs, and eat with faces close
To their plates. America is at work.

Look at Grandpa go to town on fried chicken,
The ketchup coughing from the bottle. The appliance
Salesman in the plaid coat knows. His sucked thumb

Is just another meat, the music a fly-noise
In a cracked speaker, and the mop the Negro handles
The slosh in the belly. Appliance guy pulls

At his pants, pays, and pays again when he turns
To the glazed donuts sweating behind glass.
A moist hand grabs one, no two,

For the sweet drive three blocks home.

WORRY AT THE END OF THE MONTH

The perfect life overturns like a red wagon.
My wife is doing her nails.
Her breasts are heavy, she is late,
And I'm pacing up and down like a mad doctor.

Now I see it all:
A baby fat as a waterbottle

Swaddled in a blue blanket.
Is he smiling for Grandma's Kodak?
Is he burping the milk of pleasure?
Is he kicking his feet for song?
No, he's grunting with one hand on my nose.

Adios to my Italian clothes,
My rack of wines, my dear friends,
My car glinting evilness on the front bumper,
The crown of cleverness on my head deflating like a cake.

Adios to my weekend trips,
Pacific Grove where, behind the finely ground lenses
Of German binoculars, the sea is blue as a made-up heaven;
Where whales sing, tourists look,
And the three-flavored ice cream cones totter
In our hands
As we go from shop to shop.

The good life ends.
Evenings I will stay home
And watch the fireplace with its saw of red flames,
My daughter reading, my wife reading,
My pitbull Apollo cleaning a paw,
With Dinner Jazz on the radio,
Piano noise like the footsteps of a divorced man
Walking up stairs. I will stare
At my bank book, worry my brow into lines,
And rinse my throwaway shaver over and over.

Now what will my daughter say?
Cry? Lecture me on self-control?
Conspire with Apollo, heathen dog
Who, I know in my heart, has always eyed
My leg as a second helping of Mexican food.

I'm too old to start over. The hair
On my pillow could smother a kingly rat.

My brow is lined, my bones a wobbly chair.
Give a week, a month, he'll be here,
Bundle that's my life, child for the next century.
Hoodlum out for my sleep, my son, my son,
Bald, pink, with fists beating sparks from my sleeping eyes.

SORROW IN FRENCH

Piaf, just what are you saying?
Three songs, sherry not yet dry
On the tongue, newspapers twisted
Into busy wreaths of fire,
And I turn to my daughter,
Little thinker on the couch.
She looks away. She doesn't want
Anything to do with failure,
These songs that don't make sense
At any speed. I go alone,
Guessing what it all means
– *poulet* is "pole" and *poulet*
Au Vinaigre is "my pole
Has many vines." I listen
At the window. The flute has told
Me more, the violin, the drum
That banged like the guillotine.
Still, I don't know enough.
I play them again.

        I close
My eyes, rest, Is it Seurat
And his river banks, or maybe
Van Gogh in yellow rooms, the
Stuff of postcards? Is it rain,
Rain and bricked streets that lead to
Adultery on a squeaky bed,
The stuff of movies? Piaf's voice

Is the giveaway, scrawny
Bird huddled on a lone wire,
Flogged by wind and bad romance.
I think I know. The sherry
Brings on the clouds, fogged-up
Lenses above my neighbor's trees,
And here, at the front window,
Sorrow is a lawnful of
Birds who, like us, share the green,
Make noises in pairs, and then,
Without so much as a word,
Go alone in the air.

TAKING THE MOVIES TO THE STREETS

The French movie star takes off her blouse,
Puts it back on. Nothing
For you Pierre,
This week,
Next week,
And if I have it my way,
As long as that dirty thing stands up.

The movie ends.
The patrons blink when the lights come on.
I help my wife with her coat;
My friend helps his wife with her coat.
The men around us are just as helpful.
Are any of them like me,
Confused about what they just saw,
Two hours of bedroom crying?
And why did the old nun beat herself with a candle?
What was this about a saint with a flying cape?
Where did the mouse come from
When the violins started?

(Poor, brie-fed mouse, ten minutes
On camera and no credit in the end.)

Outside, the stars mingle with neon,
The faces of newspapers drink from the gutter.
We walk back to the car, the four
Of us smiling. What was it
About? I look back: the marquee glows "psycho-drama."
That's what I need in life. Lust is a slow slime
In the heart. I nudge against my friend's
Wife's tear-shaped ass. She's beautiful.
I've seen her hang laundry and board a bus
In high heels. "Psycho-drama," I breathe
In her ear. She squeals, laughs, and tells
Her husband, "Honey, he's doing it again!"
Honey punches me in the arm,
Softly. "Psycho-drama," he says,
And places a creepy kiss on my screaming wife's mouth.

ROUGH TRANSLATION OF A SABINE'S POEM

It's not the night's fault.
The violins have tried to make the shirts,
Still hung on the wires, get up and find bodies.
It's no one's fault that the chic are gone.
A man with no legs is propped up in a doorway –
Teddy bear legs, cut off at the knees.
I shake a sweaty coin in his hands.
Later his nephew will come to take him home,
Maybe carry him under his arm like a box,
Maybe let him stand on his shoulders,
A circus act taken to the streets.

In the windows the mannequins are stiff as ever –
If you were to knock on them with a knuckle,

Dust would cry from their eyes,
They're bored of standing bent just so.
I'm like a mannequin. The dust of boredom
Weeps from my eyes, sprays from nostrils,
Jumps from my hair. I'm dust inside, dust
Of boredom and cars that breathed on me for years.

I have nothing to pass on, to tell a son.
It's easy to poke a hole in snow,
Easy to drive a car with two hands, drink
With your mouth, sleep with your eyes closed.
But how does this knowledge help?
It won't earn a diploma, certainly not make money,
And money is what he'll need to support my dreams,
Women with their breasts like a handful of sand.

A horse of smells. I look back.
It's the man with no legs. He's pushing himself
Toward me on a rickety platform of skates.
I hurry away, only to stumble
Into his blind cousin, sores the color of bacon.
I offer coins, and one to a grandma in shawl,
Two to a boy with a face of black smoke.

I enter a bar called Over the Skies of Acapulco.
The talk there is like digestion,
Quiet then suddenly loud.
After one drink I leave
Because the man on the squeaky stool next to me
Is speaking about his wife, no his lover,
His wife's first lover.

Why any of this?
The poor who envy the rich,
And the rich who despise the lonely,
The lonely in love with cereal that floats.
I'm getting the hell out.

I'm going to take these hands that work best
While I'm asleep. And some clothes.
The forest is green and made up of air.

ARS POETICA, OR MAZATLAN, ON A DAY WHEN BODIES
WASH TO THE SHORE

The body's in the morgue,
And the morgue's on this street
Where we're standing, Omar and I,
Invisible to the taxis and the mules
And the sleeping dogs
In the train station's shadow.

Earlier, we were at the *mercado,*
With its upside-down chickens
Blinking blood from all holes.
(We bought lemons and made bitter faces at oranges.)
Earlier, we were throwing down coins
In restaurants, big shots from
The North, because our hearts were full
And our wallets sandwiches for the dancing poor.

Now we're not so sure.
It's death that rode in with the waves
While we stood ankle-deep,
Backs toward the shore, the sky slashed
White where the blue would not go.
Death is the body of a man
With his arms forced into bent Ls,
With his hair whipping his eyes for not seeing,
With his belly, half of the world the ant can't climb.

Now we're not so sure.
The heat shimmers the leaves on the trees.

The taxis are asleep at jammed meters
And the children, once busy with balls,
Are eating the caked ice cream along their arms.
The truth is, we want to go home,
Vanish in the train's white smoke,
And miraculously find ourselves
In America. Omar, I ask, have you had enough?
He raises his face to mine,
Taps a cigarette against a yellow thumb
And strikes a blue flame.

No, we can't go. Our business
Is unfinished. I know this; Omar knows this.
We'll clomp down like mules to the shore,
Test the water with a hoof, and walk in
Until our heads bob on water, are covered by water.
If we come up, our teeth will flash signals
To those who've gathered –
Stout man, two old mothers, kids and their bikes.
We live! We live! Crabs, with snapping claws,
Race to where they think we may wash
To the shore, legs first.

HOME COURSE IN RELIGION

I miss not eating fish on Friday,
The halved lemon squeezed a third time around,
And our prayers, silent mutters
To God, whom we knew, whom we trusted
To make things right. I miss the incense,
White scarf of smoke. I miss Monsignor Singleton
Saying Mass in Latin with his back to us.
When he raised the Host, I looked down,
Usually at my hands, which were pink like the underside
Of a starfish. I miss the nuns, and the chalk smells
Of popped erasers, and the peppery corduroy
That *swished* when we walked. I never understood
The Trinity, and still have doubts,
But was happy for the Father, Son, and Holy Ghost.
I miss Sister Maria, her white-dove skin,
And the pagan babies waiting for our candles.
My favorite country was Italy, the boot country.
The Pope lived there in his purple cape,
And Venice was a flood of fishless canals.
Europe made me dream a lot. I wished my town
Were water, not dry lawns and thirsty kids.
I also like France, which was Catholic,
And England, which was not Catholic
But green and cool like the insides of trees.
I miss walking home in my Catholic clothes.
I miss crossing myself when an ambulance raced its siren.
At home a crucifix hung in almost every room,
Holy water in the cupboard behind the jam
And a box of pretzels. The Bible
Weighed less than our medical dictionary,
Where the dead lay with toes poking through white sheets.
Palm-leaf crosses withered in the kitchen window
For our Okie neighbors to look at in awe.

Okies are now the homeless, car salesmen,
And waitresses. The pagan babies are the simple poor,

The nuns in their sleds of black shadow
Women with skirts up to their knees.
Our school, condemned by the city, now creaks
With mice, not the polished shoes of Catholicism.
In school, I didn't mean to be bad.
I wrote I WILL NOT TALK BACK a lot of times
On the blackboard, and some of that dust
Worked into my soul. Now I'm quiet,
The telephone is quiet, my family
And the people I like best are quiet.
The nuns would be proud of me,
And so would Monsignor Singleton,
Who once begged me to please be quiet in the confessional.
But Monsignor, I can't help talking.
The Church is changed. We have folksy guitars
And an electric bass to thump our hearts, croissants
Instead of donuts, and three kinds of coffee,
Juice if you want. There are more lawyers
Than ever, doctors, teachers, and the educated
Looking for a way out. There are retreats,
Young Adult groups, spaghetti dinners
For parents without partners,
Five-mile runs for priests and nuns,
Lay ministry, fewer bingo nights, more poor people
Cuddling newspapers over warm grates of steam.
Monsignor, good priest who stared holiness
Into my body, the church on Pine Street is in trouble:
At the altar of Mary, we have electric bulbs,
Not candles, sitting in the votive cups.
You drop a quarter
Into the slot and a single bulb comes on.
With more quarters, with more sins notching the soul,
The altar lights up like a pinball machine.
How do we kneel and pray at such a place?
Monsignor, come back, with a holy sleight of hand,
With the smoke, the wavering flame,
The glow of the votive cup like a red taillight,
The teary melt of wax.

THE GOLD CANNON

Grown-ups didn't know more than me
About the dead. I'd ask, Do you really have to stay
There? and they would say, It's up to God.
Now that Father was dead I wondered
About him a lot. He was there,
But also in heaven, as my grandmother said.
I wanted to ask, How can he be in two places?
But knew better. I would lower my eyes
And remember Father's favorite shirt hung
On a shovel two days before he died.

I thought about heaven in a different way
From other kids. At the cemetery there was a cannon,
And every time we drove through the cement gate
I would get on my knees in the back seat
Of our Chevy and peek at the gold-painted cannon.
I thought the last thing a dead person did
Was stick his head in the barrel. An angel
Would help give the neck a little twist,
And then you were really dead. There was one cannon,
Like one God, and graves rolled on a hill,
Then over that hill, then up again.

APPLE

I open the orange photo album
And they're there, family in black and whites,
Off-color prints. I like the one of
My brother, sister, and me standing by a car
Fender. We're like bushes set not quite straight
In the ground, thin and crooked, and we are shading
Our eyes in childish salutes. The shadow
Of our mother behind the camera
Is lean. The ground at our feet is sandy.

126

The houses behind us are white, rickety white
From thirty years of rain. I like this
Photograph, circa 1956. We were new
In our bodies and the people we loved were still alive.
My uncle had a Model-T that I tried to help
Get started. Instead of pushing, I pulled
From the front fender and was dragged up the alley,
The engine whirring warm air into my face. My uncle
Stopped, pulled me up, swatted a cloud
Of dust from my pants. My brother
Was tricking me then, too.
He would say, Captain Kangaroo
Lives in that house,
And of course I would climb the brick steps and knock.
He would point, That kid said you were black,
And I would pick up the nearest rock.
I didn't catch on right away
That meanness was part of the family.
I kept going where people told me to go.
One day my mother sent me to Charlie's Market
For an apple pie, the kind in which one end peeks
From a sleeve of waxed paper. I gave Charlie
The fifteen cents. I started
Home staring at the end of the apple pie,
Little snout of sugary crust.
I wanted very badly to take one bite.
I walked slowly thinking, Just one bite.
Mother would say, You had yours without asking
But you should wait next time.
She wouldn't be too mad. I worried
About the apple pie, walked slowly
Around the block the long way,
And when I couldn't stand it anymore,
I took a bite. A sugary flake fell from my mouth.
It was sweet. I took a second bite
And three lines worried my brow.
I took the pie out of the paper
Wrapper, and turned it the other way

So the eaten side didn't show.
But I kept walking around the block, a kid
Lost in a neighborly orbit, and staring
At the pie. Again I couldn't stand it.
My mouth opened when my hand
Forced the pie to my face.
Now both sides were ruined,
Chunks gone out. How could I say,
Mom, I don't know how it got that way.
I hid in a vacant lot
Behind a stack of greenish boards,
Companion to the scurry of red ants at my feet.
I don't remember ever getting up to go back home.

Laughter is another sin. How funny
To think I could eat from both ends
And get away with it. God *is* at least that voice
Inside us that says *yes* and *no.*
God said *no,* and I hid behind a stack
Of boards. God said *yes* when
I tried to help Uncle with his old black car
And didn't let me die under a dusty wheel.
It's been that way ever since. Yes
And no, never a maybe. Because of this,
I once tried to steal from Charlie's Market.
I stood at a tier of thirteen kinds of candy,
And I closed my hand around a Baby Ruth,
Then opened it very quickly
Because it was wrong. I was a boy,
No brighter than the penny
In my pocket. I closed my hand around
The candy again, then opened it.
God would know, my mother would know,
And certainly Charlie who was leaning his elbows
On the glass counter. I didn't see him watching.
My small eyes stared at the candy,
First temptation of the greedy tooth.

My hand opened and closed around the Baby Ruth
Several more times. I kept thinking
All I have to do is pick it up
And it'll be mine.

THE DICTIONARIES
for Christopher Buckley

Disease happened overnight, just when you thought you
Were going to make the baseball team.
At the stove, Mother with steamed-up glasses
Said you couldn't count your chickens,
Then wiped her hands and set the medical dictionary
In my lap – ringworm and a Chinese boy
In the iron lung made me sit up.
On another page, a row of eyeballs,
Some pink, some red and droopy,
Some gray because one side of the boy was dead.
This was a new one to me. I closed the dictionary
And the next day at school I remembered
The boy, the eyeballs, a mouth with its cave of sores,
Ringworms and cancer. I licked my pencil
And did math on my fingers and was beginning
To think that maybe disease made me bad at math.
At home in my bedroom I looked up
And down my arms and thought about the dead.
Sometimes I would press a flashlight
Against my palm and scare myself
Because I could see the blood,
Bright as a red scarf. My brother would
Look at his blood and I would look at mine,
And both of us would eat all our food.
Just before Advent we started learning religion.
One morning Sister told us about the Trinity,
Then told us to draw pictures of them.

I got confused because I couldn't figure them out
And drew three gray crosses, one taller than the next.
Sister yelled at me, pinched my shoulder,
And that night I decided to look
In our Catholic dictionary to see
About the Trinity. It said,
The mystery whereby God, while being numerically one,
Exists in three divine Persons. I was perplexed
Because that was only one religious word.
On the same page there were fifteen others,
On the next page there were twelve,
And sooner or later I would have to know
Them all. Right below *Trinity* was *Triple Candlestick,*
Which was easy. I memorized:
A candlestick so formed that three separate
Candles arise from one base. At dinner
I told Mother about the Triple Candlestick,
Potato in mouth. She was proud,
She said, and the next day at school
I waited for Sister to ask about the Triple Candlestick.
But she said again. Now draw the Trinity,
Which I thought was something like
People inside each other
And was somehow like manners.
Sometimes you could act one way at a friend's house,
But at your grandmother's house you had to act
Another way. I drew three faces, one larger than the next,
All looking pretty happy
But not so happy that they were smiling
And showing their teeth. Sister licked a blue star
Of approval and let me monitor the bad boys at lunch.
At home, I felt light and holy.
I got the can of marbles
That Uncle got us after Father died,
And poured them on the floor in the empty bedroom.
With the sweep of my hand, the marbles jumped up the walls,
Ricocheted and clattered. My brother joined me,

Then my sister, and all of us went wild making the marbles
Jump. When mother came home, we stopped.
Before dinner I peeked at the medical dictionary,
Lung sitting in a white pan. After dinner I looked
At the Catholic dictionary. I knew *Triple Candlestick*
And *Trinity.* On the same page
Was *Tre Ore.* I went to bed saying
Over and over, A devotion commemorating
The three hours' agony of Christ
On the cross. This was second grade, winter,
A year of troubled math and disease,
God the Trinity, with bleeding palms and redemptive heart.

SOME MYSTERIES

I was pretty holy by third grade. Mother could see that,
And could see that I had given up stealing butt-faced plums
And walking with Pepsi cans smashed onto my shoes.
Sundays, she gave me a quarter for
The wicker basket, smoothed my hair with water
And let me go. I sat in the front pew,
Among old Italian women hunched together
Like pigeons, happy because it was only a matter
Of time before Monsignor would say, We are sinners.
I would look at my shoes
And nod my head Yes. I recalled my sins.
Years before I tossed a hairbrush
Into my sister's panties. It was a game in our bedroom,
Doctor Doctor, and for me the hairbrush
Resembled a doctor's tool.
I opened her panties and said, This should help – buzzzzzz.
While we played Mother came in with her apron of chickens,
And said, Alex is having a party –
Alex the boy whose hand
Traveled both ways in the wringer/washer.

Sister and I were scared because we thought mother saw.
She didn't. She wrung her hands into the apron,
Said, Wash your faces. I went to the bathroom
And hurt myself with hot water – the handles of
The faucets were confusing. I couldn't see sister.
I held onto the tub and blinked until
My eyesight returned. I then saw the brush
Wagging in her panties as mother prodded us
To the car. Sometime between
Our house and Alex's house, between childhood
And her older years, she got it out, that and more.
In church I would remember my sins and smile,
Then feel bad for remembering such moments.
When Mass was over and the donuts eaten,
I stood outside admiring the stained-glass windows
Breathing in light – the crucified Jesus
Was blood red at twenty to noon. I felt bad for Him
But much better when I turned away. I liked the walk home,
And liked when I passed the rectory: behind the thorny wall
Thumping sounds like a soccer ball,
Which made me wonder what our nuns did on weekends.
I would listen for a while, then leave,
Thinking that maybe this is what mystery was,
That you hear a *thump* and have to guess
What it is. I guessed a soccer ball
And saw Sister Marie running around the yard.
Monsignor's hands were pressed together in prayer,
His eyes like the floating eyes of the saints
On the church ceiling. I had a lot of ideas back then,
And liked to walk around. *Thump* was mystery,
A ball against the wall, and after Mass,
After the Host cleaned you up, a scoreless game.

SOME WORRY

In second grade I still had to stand far away
From the urinal to get my pee in.
This made me nervous. I opened myself up
To bacteria and dust swirling in the shafts of sunlight.
I worried more and more about disease.
I was still looking at the medical dictionary
And staring at the Chinese boy in
His iron lung. We became friends.
I would open the dictionary
And by habit the book fell open to his face.
I looked at him, and more than once I grew scared
Because I thought it was my face in the iron lung picture
And if I closed the book I might go away.
I worried about not feeling enough.
Sometimes when I prayed my shoulders tingled,
And other times I only felt the rub of cloth. Sister Marie
Said glorious things happen when boys and girls
Were sincere. I thought maybe I
Had forgotten to confess all my sins,
And thought maybe because some of my pee
Fell on the ground God was keeping me from feeling.
This scared me. Feeling was one of five senses,
And if you didn't feel that meant you only had
Four other senses and there was no telling
When you might go blind, or one of your best friends
Might shoot a cap gun in both your ears.
Of course I could cry. What I wanted to return
Was that tingle in my shoulders. For about eight years
I didn't feel too much, and worried a lot.
My eyesight was failing and sometimes I had difficulty
Hearing the teacher talk about the Euphrates.
One summer, when I was sixteen,
Feeling slowly came back to my shoulders
And my face began to turn red when relatives
Fumbled in their pockets for dimes

And said, Gary, you've grown tall. At first
I thought I was getting sick and became
Very suspicious of people who didn't wash their hands.
Then I realized I was becoming more in tune
With people. I got to thinking that maybe
This is how a saint feels when he's about
To do something really nice. By this time
I had stopped praying,
And the Christ in our bedroom began to glow
Later and later. But my feelings returned.
I got in the habit of
Walking around and singing
Made-up prayers. The trees seemed special.
The old Armenian neighbor took a long time
To wave but eventually he
Stopped his raking to raise a hand.
At school, my grades improved.
I was startled when I recognized a verb in a sentence
And began to think that maybe teachers were
Onto something after all. I would read,
The Euphrates, a mighty river that replenished
The Persian Empire time and time again,
Is a mile wide at more than twenty junctions.
Always when I got to the verb *is,*
My face burned a little and I became happy.
I realized learning was a bodily thing,
That you could read a really important book
And knowledge would spread into your face and your chest.
I began to walk slower in
The hallways, no longer embarrassed
About poor grades. I began to recognize the
Smart kids because none of them rushed around
A lot. Since I was now among them
This made me feel OK about myself. My shoulders tingled.
My face turned red for every class except algebra,
Which was still, $x = \dfrac{-b \pm \sqrt{b^2 - 4ac}}{2a}$

But by my senior year these feelings left me.
When I looked at a verb, my face didn't respond.
The words to prayers seemed silly,
And trees that were once special didn't move so much.
Once, in an abandoned house, I almost cried
Because the wallpaper was peeling,
And a really sad orange, blue from being forgotten,
Was on the floor and not even the ants bothered with it.
The Venetian blinds were the kind that hung
In our house on Braly Street,
And no matter how I pulled on the chain
I couldn't straighten them. The rooms were crooked
With shadows. The refrigerator blazed with flies
And the festering mold of peaches crawled in a cardboard box.
I went room to room strangling wire coat hangers.
Something was wrong. On my way back
Home, I realized that the Chinese boy
In the iron lung was dead. His lungs, vest of
Sorrow, were shredding apart in the black earth.

THE BOX FAN

For nine months the box fan held its breath
In the closet. For three months of summer
It rattled the pages
Of *TV Guide*. It was summer now.
My stepfather was drinking Jack Daniels
From a TV tray pressed with the faces
Of our dead and live presidents.
The trouble with you,
He said, is that you don't respect the law.
He had come home from work, fingers black
From book print, the fissures of paper cuts
On the web of skin
Between thumb and index finger.

I had chained my bike to a tree.
He said there were laws against that kind
Of behavior. It hurt the tree. It was an eyesore.
Babies would poke an eye out on the handlebars
And could take away our house.

The sour heat of bourbon cracked the ice.
The pages rattled in the whir of the fan,
Blades the color of spoons and forks falling
From a drawer. I knew
It would take more than a knife to bring him down,
More than a slammed door to jam his heart.
You see my point? he said,
And then asked me to spell *implements,*
A word he picked up from *TV Guide.*
While I spelled the word,
While I counted out the letters
On my fingers, he drained his bourbon,
The sliver of ice riding in the thick chute of throat.
He poured himself another and said,
I like that. I-m-p-l-e-m-e-n-t-s.
It's a good word to know.
He fixed the fan so that my hair stirred
And the pages of the magazine ruffled
From Sunday to Friday. I saw a serious face,
Then a laughing face in those pages,
Ads for steam cleaning and miracle products,
And the shuffle of my favorite nighttime shows.
He said that the trouble with me,
With a lot of young people, is that we can't spell.
He poured an inch of bourbon, with no ice,
And said, Try it again, without your fingers –
I imagined the fan blades and blood jumping to the wall.

I had no choice but to shave my hair
And wrestle – thirty guys humping one another
On a mat. I didn't like high school.
There were no classes in archeology,
And the girls were too much like flowers
To bother with them. My brother, I think,
Was a hippie, and my sister, I know,
Was the runner-up queen of the Latin American Club.
When I saw her in the cafeteria, waved
And said things like, Debbie, is it your turn
To do the dishes tonight? she would smile and
Make real scary eyes. When I saw my brother
In his long hair and sissy bell-bottom pants,
He would look through me at a little snotty
Piece of gum on the ground. Neither of them
Liked me. So I sided with the wrestling coach,
The same person who taught you how to drive.
But first there was wrestling, young dudes
In a steamy room, and coach with his silver whistle,
His clipboard, his pencil behind his clubbed ear.
I was no good. Everyone was better
Than me. Everyone was larger
In the showers, their cocks like heavy wrenches,
Their hair like the scribbling of a mad child.
I would lather as best I could to hide
What I didn't have, then walk home
In the dark. When we wrestled
Madera High, I was pinned in twelve seconds.
My Mom threw me a half stick of gum
From the bleachers. She shouted, It's Juicy Fruit!
And I just looked at her. I looked at
The three spectators, all crunching corn nuts,
Their faces like punched-in paper bags.
We lost that night. The next day in Biology
I chewed my half stick of Juicy Fruit

And thought about what can go wrong
In twelve seconds. The guy who pinned
Me was named Bloodworth, a meaningful name.
That night I asked Mom what our name meant in Spanish.
She stirred crackling *papas* and said it meant Mexican.
I asked her what was the worst thing that happened
To her in the shortest period
Of time. She looked at my stepfather's chair
And told me to take out the garbage.
That year I gained weight, lost weight,
And lost more matches, nearly all by pins.
I wore my arm in a sling when
I got blood poisoning from a dirty fingernail.
I liked that. I liked being hurt. I even went so far
As limping, which I thought would attract girls.

One day at lunch the counselor called me to his office.
I killed my sandwich in three bites. In his
Office of unwashed coffee mugs,
He asked what I wanted from life.
I told him I wanted to be an archeologist,
And if not that, then an oceanographer.
I told him that I had these feelings
I was Chinese, that I had lived before
And was going to live again. He told me
To get a drink of water and that by fifth period
I should reconsider what I was saying.
I studied some, dated once, ate the same sandwich
Until it was spring in most of the trees
That circled the campus, and wrestling was over.
Then school was over. That summer I mowed lawns,
Picked grapes, and rode my bike
Up and down my block because it was good
For heart and legs. The next year I took Driver's Ed.
Coach was the teacher. He said, Don't be scared
But you're going to see some punks
Getting killed. If you're going to cry,

Do it later. He turned on the projector,
A funnel of silver light that showed motes of dust,
Then six seconds of car wreck from different angles.
The narrator with a wrestler's haircut came on.
His face was thick like a canned ham
Sliding onto a platter. He held up a black tennis shoe.
He said, The boy who wore this sneaker is dead.
Two girls cried. Three boys laughed.
Coach smiled and slapped the clipboard
Against his leg, kind of hard.
With one year of wresting behind me,
I barely peeked but thought,
Six seconds for the kid with the sneakers,
Twelve seconds for Bloodworth to throw me on my back.
Tough luck in half the time.

DRINKING IN THE SIXTIES

Drinking made you popular at school,
And laughing while you drank
Made you friends. I noticed teachers
Laughed when they carried armfuls of books.
I began to think that they were drunk.
I noticed Mrs. Tuttle seldom kept her legs together,
Lipstick overrunning her mouth. Coach knew only
So many words. The dean's hand trembled
When he tried to open doors. Our English teacher
Kept repeating, A noun is a person, place, or thing.
You students are a noun, Fresno is a noun,
Bobbie's chair is a noun. Cheerleaders
Were pretty happy when thrown into the air.
Scott and I got a brown quart of beer
And sat in an abandoned house at dusk –
The walls were kicked open to chalk
Where rednecks banged heads.

We kept peering out the broken front window
And saying things like, Fuckin' narcs,
When we heard faraway voices. I sucked the old air
Of peeling wallpaper
And swigged beer with one eye on Scott.
I told him about the Chinese boy in the iron lung –
Vest of blood, milky skin of nothing to do.
You can live that way, with a hand mirror
To look around corners.
Scott swigged the quart and said,
Some rivers peter out before they get to the sea.
I swigged the quart and said that people
With long hair don't laugh as hard –
Except if they're a woman or a clean-cut hippie.
I walked to the window, cursed, Fuckin' queers,
And Scott with all his strength bent a wire hanger.
I liked the shape of it, and beat a board
Against the wall, chalky dust smothering the good air.
Scott kicked a greenish orange, dead of all sweetness,
Of rain and the bitter seeds.
I kicked the stove. I pulled a calendar from
The kitchen wall. The couch didn't mean
Much when slashed with a screwdriver.
We trashed that already trashed house,
And then we were sorry. Scott's hands
Were black. My armpits flooded with worry
And sweat. I slammed the quart, and thought of school:
Mrs. Tuttle's thighs and the cheerleaders cartwheeling
For a last-place team. Coach was farting softly
Into his bedsheets,
And the dean's hand was on the throat
Of his stinky dog. His wife smelled. His house was
Festering in lousy paint. Scott kicked the
Living room walls, and because I was seventeen
And acne bit my throat in three places,
I brought chair down on chair –
Splinters of wood flying at the windows.

Outside, we threw ourselves on a grave of leaves,
Groaning under the chipped moon's laughter.

THE LEVEE

At seventeen, I liked driving around,
Breaking the backs of leaves and casting long shadows
Where the lawns were burned. I didn't like home,
Especially in summer. But eventually I returned to watch
My stepfather eat fried chicken on a TV tray.
He ate for bulk, not taste,
And every night he drank to flood the hole inside him.
I couldn't believe my life. I was a Mexican
Among relatives with loud furniture. I knew most
Of us wouldn't get good jobs, some
Would die, others pull over
On the sides of roads to fix their Nova Super Sports
For a hundred years. I wanted out
Because the TV wouldn't stop until eleven.
The summer heat billowed near the ceiling.
Flies mingled among the smells
Of pried-apart chicken wings. I sweated
When I drank water from a dirty glass. I thought of
Putting my fingers in the box fan, of standing up
Nails under the tires of our neighbor's car.
That's why at night I drove to the levee
And played the radio. The water
Was constant, and the blown tires that bumped along
On a filthy current no longer surprised me.
The bushes breathed dust and hamburger wrappers,
The faint stink of dead birds. After a while
I talked to myself because the songs on the radio
Didn't seem honest. I was tired of home,
Of our TV wreathed in doilies
And the glow-in-the-night Christ on the windowsill.

I was sickened by the sound of toads flopping
In the dark, of a dying fish gasping among reeds.
I began to realize that we deserved each other,
Son to his stepfather, daughter to her real mother.
That it would take more than a car to make us happy.
We deserved this life, where a canal rushed
Black water, and the stars held for a while,
Then washed away as tires floated by in twos.

NOT MOVING

Sometimes I would stub my toe on our La-Z-Boy recliner,
And mother, at her ironing board,
Sprinkling fingers of water from a saucepan,
Would say, God punished you. Scissors fell,
Splayed with angry light, and nicked my calf.
Mother was at the sink stirring the mush of
Starch for blue work shirts with black under the arms.
God punished you, she said, not looking up,
Not reaching for the mercurochrome.
My bike kicked up dirt when I fell,
And again I was punished – the bitterness of a rosebush
Biting through skin. Mother rolled down her
Window of our Dodge. God is making you pay, she said,
And then said, I'm going to buy milk.
The Dodge pulled away, stirring up the evil dust
Of leaves that won't die through any kind of rain,
And I walked home for circle Band-Aids. My brother
Stood under a tree and a pine cone fell
From a tree and ruined his eye for three weeks.
A screwdriver punctured his leg. Scalding water splashed
His foot. Spiders crawled into a pant leg,
Bites like Braille he scratched
At night. Mother woke and stood in the doorway
With her cream of white medicine.

God punished, she said. It's time to eat.
Our ill luck couldn't stop our playing.
Cats dropped from roofs and lived.
Kids did the same, rolling like bales of hay,
And laughing with flakes of grass in their spiky hair.
I did the same,
And for one summer I had to sit on a porch –
My leg was hurt from the jump. My eyes as well.
I stared into a fan and everything dried
That makes the eyeball work.

Now I don't move so fast. I read in one room,
Eat in another. The front window is dust
With a geranium bush that wags against the glass –
Unlike the rose, its petals don't bite.
The scissors are sheathed in an oily cloth.
The screwdriver hangs on a wall.
Mother is in another town.
With her fingers still dipping into a saucepan,
Her iron pouting steam and hatred for collars.
Of course, God is here, at the level of trees,
At this hour of gnats circling bruised fruit on a limb.
His beard is long and the story the same.
I'm not moving from this chair,
From this life that could pick up a hammer
And hurt on the third strike.

HOME COURSE IN RELIGION

By the time I was eighteen and in junior college
Religion was something like this: *The notion
Of "project" is an ambiguous substitute for the notion
Of quiddity, and that situation is
An ambiguous substitute for the notion of an
Objective condition resulting from the causes*

And natures interacting in the world. That was
The first sentence in a really long book.
I figured that the second sentence had
To be more difficult, and the third almost impossible,
On and on. The back of the book had impressive
Things to say. The author, a French scholar,
Got the Pope to say a few words, and one cardinal
I had heard about remarked, *Celebrated thought.*
Best Sellers said, *It ought to be read by anyone*
Who has had a formal or home-study course in metaphysics . . .
I read a chapter, then played basketball to get air
Back into my brain so I wouldn't feel so sleepy.
I returned home, sweaty in every hole,
And picked up a book that sounded like this:
Costly grace confronts us as a gracious call
To follow Jesus; it comes as a word of
Forgiveness to the broken spirit
And the contrite heart. This was clearer,
But after ten pages the good air in my brain was used up,
And I fell asleep with cracker crumbs
On my mouth. That night
My brother and I, and our two roommates, ate Top Ramen.
After dinner we tape recorded our thoughts
About Nixon, who was in a lot of trouble with Watergate.
We played it back and laughed for a long time
Because none of us understood what the other
Was saying. Some of it sounded like this:
Nixon won't confess
About the submarines or the money. Did you see how
He picked up that dog by its ears? No, that
Was Johnson. That's not the point. The certainty
Of life comes to an end. That Nixon!
People with big cars don't know how much it hurts.
Furthermore, if you realize the predicament
Then what's there to say, etc.

In bed I read four pages about a French mystic,
Who lived a common life until lightning struck

Her shoulder, then she began to talk in weird
Ways and no longer reached people with her thoughts.
The next morning I ate cereal
In my Top Ramen bowl. During P.E.
I understood more about life than with the help
Of a book. My karate instructor said,
Pain doesn't exist. Do you see
Pain when you get hit? Pain is in the mind.
The mind is the spiritual nature
That follows your body, etc. Then he matched us
By height and rank, and for twenty minutes
Let us kick and punch one another really hard.
By the time I got back to the apartment I thought
My instructor was wrong. With my one good eye
I could see the pain: red welts on my chest,
And two on my back from running away.

The Bible was much clearer. Jesus said,
O faithless and perverse generation, how long
Am I to be with you and bear with you? Bring
Your son here. Then I started on my roommate's book
About the Zen master Xu Yun. I was curious how
He could go three years eating only grass
And pine needles. I asked that about myself,
Seeing that I was living on Top Ramen and cold cereal
And oranges that rolled our way when we weren't looking.
That night my girlfriend came
Over with a large jar of peanut butter,
A present that we tried on our last three crackers.
After she left I prayed in my bedroom,
Then crossed myself so that my fingertips
Pushed into my flesh. I then started *The Problem of Evil,*
Which was clearer than my previous readings
Except when I ran into passages like this:
Oderunt peccare mali formidine poenae, oderunt peccare
Boni virtutis amore. I read nine pages
Before I fell asleep. The next morning
While I ate cereal from my Top Ramen bowl

I read a paragraph that said this: *Animal suffering?*
Their rate of production demands the existence
Of carnivorousness. But they are not dissatisfied
With life. They do not realize that they
Are suffering, they simply suffer, etc.
In Anthropology, I learned about the Papuan people.
In Geography, we discussed the uses of pumice.
I took notes but mostly watched the teacher,
Sweat stinking up his eyebrows.

When Mom called to yell at us that night,
I told her that Rick and I were three years short
Of earning good money. She said that as long
As we didn't go to prison she would be
Proud of us. Prison wasn't what I was thinking,
And God knows what I was thinking
When I picked up the book *What Is Man?*
I had to keep looking at the cover to remind me
What I was reading. Some more good air
Left my brain, and I woke only when
My girlfriend came over with a bag of oranges.
We sat on the couch. Her blouse held a lot
Of shadows, and one was my hand. I liked
That very much, and liked how her mouth fit mine.
She said that she was lonely
When I wasn't around. I said that people feel
Like that because they don't know themselves.
I said just be mellow, just think of
Yourself as a flower, etc.
When I placed my hand on her thigh, she opened her legs
Just a little, warmth that was a spooky liquid
When one of my biggest fingers crawled in.
She pushed me away, lipstick overrunning her mouth,
Her hair like the hair you wear when
You wake up from a hard sleep. After she left,
I read in the Bible
About Jesus touching each of his four wounds –

Thomas was not around when Jesus walked through the wall.
I began to feel ashamed because my left hand
Turning the pages was the hand that had snapped
Her panties closed. I got up from the couch
And washed that hand, stinky trout that I took to bed.
It was then, on a night of
More Top Ramen and a cat-and-dog storm,
I realized I might be in the wrong line of belief.

THE FAMILY IN SPRING

Family won't go away. I keep pulling up to them,
Brown faces inside a steamy station wagon.
When I was a boy my uncle flipped pennies
And let me lose, then gave them to me,
Small pile with no sack. I've done the same.
At my nephew's first communion party
I let him close his eyes and choose three times
From my wallet. Two singles is what he got, and a five.
I like my nephew. He missed the twenty and ten.
I talked with my mother, who is like those pennies
And bills, bitter with the acid of fingers.
Grandma is ill, she told me three times.
I told her I was doing OK only once.
I told her I had gone to New York. Carolyn
And I had painted the hallway
And put up new curtains. The cat ran
Away and our second car, the Chevy, was up on blocks.
This was a son speaking to his mother,
Son with the stilts of childhood not pulled down.
We sat and watched the leaves on a tree,
Fiddled with our napkins. Mariko
Brought me three inches of punch in a paper cup.
We'll turn on each other in smaller company.
I got up to leave. My family said

Their good-byes at a distance, crushed napkins
In their hands.
And went home to call in the backyard
For our lost kitten. Barney, Spike, Midnight.
We never settled on a name.
Now it was lost, a few houses away
For all we knew. When the cat didn't come,
I looked at the Chevy that was droopy eyed from
A wreck, and slammed the hood shut.
I then took my family to dinner because my nephew
Pulled the wrong bills.

That was last April. The weather then is
Today's weather, blue with some wind and leaves.
April or September, I sometimes think
I'd like to start a new family,
Join a household of three kids, not one.
It's not a matter of love. I'm happy here,
With wife and daughter, and I could
Also be happy elsewhere. I suppose
I want more, and I suppose
I'm wrong in the head. How strange,
But for years I didn't wear my wedding band,
And now it's on my finger, wink of light.
Now I'm noticing rings. It's the left hand,
The wink of gold, that says you're married,
That and the two kids in the car,
And the car itself, which is plain,
Or if not plain, then the color white.
A few weeks ago at Safeway I watched a woman
Write out a check for a great pile of groceries.
The wink was there, and a daughter, maybe thirteen,
A little older perhaps, with just enough
Purple dye in her hair to make her OK at school.
I bought my tuna, milk, and a head of lettuce,
And hurried out in time to see them pull away.
The car was a plain white Honda.

Even in the parking lot, the woman's eyes
Were on the dashboard, careful about going too fast.

My wife is a Japanese Methodist.
I went on a retreat with her only last Saturday
Where the woman in the white Honda showed up.
Her ring finger winked a star of gold.
When everyone's finger winked,
I knew I was in the right place. We ate
A lot, sat in lounge chairs, talked baseball scores.
No one complained. No one talked out of line,
Drank too much, or bragged. I liked these people.
They were kind and good, and sensible.
I thought, The one with the white Honda
Is nicer than me. All of them are nicer than me.
For a moment I felt a glow inside,
The blush of happiness with my second beer,
And was helping with the barbecue when I began
To realize that I would never be
As nice as they. This disturbed me,
That they were nicer and didn't care
How much better they were than me.
I joined my wife who was sitting
On the lounge chair. I ate my potato salad
And looked around for a place to throw my ribs.
Guilt, then repentance, is one way to Heaven.
It's Catholic, I suppose. You have one bad thought,
Then another, and suddenly you're in the confessional
Starting over on your knees. I ate my potato salad,
Tried to like them. The Japanese are the people
Who'll get everything the second time around.
I joined the game of volleyball on a new lawn.
I was smiling too much, too little, then not at all.

SUPER-EIGHT MOVIES

Siqueiros used a machine gun on Rivera's studio,
And Diego, I guess, ran his hands through his hair.
He didn't eat for two days.
He trudged his elephant weight around the patio
And waited for Frida,
Busy primping her eyebrow,
Busy wiggling her underwear into place,
Busy with a stiff brush and her bluish wounds,
Busy blowing smoke into the face of her clapping monkey.

And Rivera, I guess, tightened his belt.
He scolded Trotsky,
Poor guy who in the end crumpled under a knife,
Just as he was sitting down to lunch
Or was it a long letter to Russia?
Imagine this:
Rivera with his bad back,
Trotsky with his bleeding fountain pen,
These two greats, and now me, little piss ant,
Crawling through the studio in San Angel.

This was Mexico in the thirties,
With rain pelting the bellies of frolicking dogs,
With the president toasting dead colonels,
With Fords squashing the juicy life out of fruit stands.

This is me in the nineties,
Me and a buddy touching the walls
Where Frida leaned and said, Fuck off, America.
Maybe she laughed with smoke in both nostrils.
Maybe she touched her one eyebrow,
Maybe she went outside, cigarette lit,
And watched pine trees bleed the moon with their needles.
They were beautifully crazy as they howled
At each other from various beds.

I've never known anyone famous.
I've never known a singer
Or an actress with tears twisted into her handkerchief.
I've never known anyone on television,
Or even a barber humming "Dos Arbolitos."
I've only known my famous aunt,
Who could cha-cha-cha with a glass of water
On her head.

I'm wild crawling through Diego and Frida's studio.
Art happened here, and love, I guess.
I sneeze the dust of years, swallowing
My chewing gum when I look up at the skylight.
I drink water and crush my paper cup.
I remember the Spanish verb "to touch."
I touch the rope that keeps me
From the wheelchair where Frida sat,
A lasso of cigarette smoke in her hair,
Dead of light for thirty years.
The floor creaks. Voices carry to the second floor,
And I have nothing to carry home but two postcards.
I'm going to lean against the wall,
And rub fame and dirt into my peasant shoulders.

QUE PRETTY IN TEJAS
para Sandra Cisneros

That on hangers her skirt sways to *rancheras,*
That the faucet drips a wink of water,
That her table wobbles,
That I rest my arm on a table and I also wobble,
That her boot falls and rights itself when she looks,
That her pillow says *mi vida* and she means it,
That this same pillow rocked the sadness from a good man,
That she kisses a napkin and says, "Here this is for you,"

That the river behind her yard is "S" shaped,
That the bronze Buddha throws up his arms to the trees,
That the blackest of black birds squeak like latches,
That she says, "Let's go," and we climb into her red truck:
Que Pretty is happy. She shifts into second,
Then third, the slant of a Texas sky in the windshield.
The radio is off, and still there is music.
From the visor, a dangling chorus line
Of Mexican saints and Virgins who didn't get away.
By fourth gear,
By the time we're tapping a beat on our thighs,
They're wiggling their skirted bottoms.

TRAVELING BURROS
for Tomás Zavala

That the long-lashed burro hauls three stones
And a pebble rides inside your shoe.
That the road is pocked with giant holes,
And smaller holes sigh inside your heart
While those you like best are home,
Feet up on the hassock, loving their lives
With Mexican chocolate. They're reading your mail,
You think, the good news from friends
And K-Mart with blue light specials.
They're listening to "An American in Paris,"
And rattling ice cubes in a tumbler.
You're rattling a cough that has no end.
You're listening to a rust-colored chicken,
Its claws filthy from crowing on top
Of the sleeping pig. It's Christmas day,
No kidding, and you're kicking up the same dust
Where Zapotec Indians pounded a hard living,
And still do, their poor souls whittled
To a stick that pokes the earth.

Whose idea was this? You could have
Stayed home and unwrapped gifts with family.
But here, beast and man, you climb
A leafy hill, the burro wagging its rocks,
And you building a greasy fire under each arm.
It doesn't take long to put two and two together,
Or add up the strength of a chicken
Flapping under a hatchet. You hear
The hatchet fall, and wince with both hands
On your ears. You rest on a fallen tree,
Get back up. You catch up to the burro,
Overtake him for a moment, then drop back.
The burro drops three stones,
The start of a house for either the dead
Or the living, some ruin tourists
Will dance on, in time. Here, it's for the living,
Exhausted in the leafy hills.

OLD PROF WITH BOTH HANDS ON THE RAIL

Now, at this age, burst veins unravel
On my nose. A cricket complains in my knee.
My hair falls when I sneeze
Or hurry up the marble steps to my class.
My profession is to pull on the beard of Whitman
And kick him awake with ideas.
Idea one, he enjoyed frolicking in grass.
Idea two, he wrote with a pencil licked by good friends.
Idea three, he raised a house with a hammer.
I cough when I say, The exam should be done in ink,
And stare down through eyeglasses,
Words like the march of ants.

I suppose the young will frolic in grass
And in a field hammer away each other's flesh,

Their sticky love bringing on a curious fox
And perhaps one or two babies.
I cough on these words,
And shiver when a student raises a hammer,
I mean a hand, and asks
If grass is a symbol or just the color green.
I cup my ear with its wheel of hairs,
And jargon gathers paste in the corners
Of my mouth. The bell rattles
My nerves. I pull myself down the rails —
My lively shadow catches up
And races ahead, where the dead books leave off.

COLLEGE CAR

At twenty, John Berryman raised a fountain pen
And flicked ink on paper. At the same age,
Under the Fresno sun, I told myself,
I could get fifty bucks for my Rambler.
The car had killed three stripeless cats
And splattered a grille of butterflies.
I thought of Berryman and my dead car.
The radiator leaked in two places,
Biblical wounds that made me touch my palms.
The windshield was cracked
Like Henry James's bowl. The torn car seat
Was a gag of cotton.
Here was Jarrell on the crushed front fender,
And here was Twain's muddy river circling
From engine block to radiator.
Here was a matchbook with Bukowski's telephone number.
Here was a crushed can on the floorboard,
And the bottle cap of its metallic sweetness.
Here was Edgar Lee Masters,
His grassy eyebrows poking around a tree.

Here was a wise-ass junior with four English classes.
I was selling my slave ship.
The radio was gone, the visor pelted with dust,
The grille like a flat-nosed shark.
I drove up the street
Past the yards hanging with fruit,
Plum that was the blood of Christ, grape
That the fox ate employing only his front teeth.
I drove to a junkyard,
Where fifty was really thirty-five,
A big seed in overalls licking his thumb
And counting them out in greasy fives.
His dog peed on my car tire and barked inches
From my crotch. I waved good-bye
And the walk home took two hours. Black birds
Pecked at glass and sand. A stinky wind
From the cement works dusted my nose,
And three rednecks stopped their Ford Pinto
To push me around. I walked through the heat
That was nothing like Moses sneaking from Egypt.
Upper division English didn't help.
It was hell itself, Mr. Dante,
Not a spiral into the earth but a flat march home.

RURAL LIVING

Firebaugh or Five Points,
Three houses clustered off Highway 152,
A Portuguese dairy farmer is settling down
To a late breakfast, the baseball game
Already on. It's eggs and potatoes mostly,
A stack of toast, some laced coffee,
Salt raining good luck on a plate.
He strikes a root-dark finger against the edge
Of the table. Cincinnati has scored three times.

A man is on second adjusting his jock for America.
How could morning end so quickly?

The farmer fills up on eggs and baseball,
And the 4-H son from Rolinda gets his fill
In the barn. He's with the farmer's heavier daughter,
And it's mostly breast, salty neck,
Some whiff of armpit where an onion could grow.
They laugh and clack their teeth together,
Sweat weeping from their bodies.
One good feel, and she pushes him away,
Hair mussed and lipstick overrunning her mouth.
The truck driver's son breathes hard,
Happily. He pushes over a tire
Where a cat sleeps. He kisses his girl,
And his girl squirms free,
Her bottom waddling like a flock of dirty geese.

Outside, at ten minutes to twelve,
The heat has sucked shadows from even the largest cows.

DIZZY GIRLS IN THE SIXTIES

Back then even the good girls got dizzy
When you dropped an aspirin into a Coke,
Spoke with an English accent,
Or flickered a cut-out photo of Paul McCartney.
They got dizzy and dropped into your arms,
Brother said. And he said two guitar chords helped,
And the theme song to *Bonanza* made them walk
Backwards and wonder about the talent
That lay under a boy's black fingernails.
I played these chords. And when I could,
I shuffled my deck of cards and said,
"Let's get naked, *esa*. I won't tell – honest."
They didn't listen. Mostly they thumbed

158

Through magazines while teasing their hair
Into a nest of trouble. By seventh grade,
I was regrouping my hormones into one hard muscle
And no longer went around with my hands
Cupped in the hollow of my arms, the intentional farts
Cutting the classroom air.
It was a hit in fourth grade
But didn't work after the Beatles docked
In the hearts of girls and young mothers.
The aspirin didn't work either,
Or the English accent from a brown face
Or the chords on a Sears guitar.
I was nowhere, really, the cafeteria helper
Scooping chile beans into a plastic dish.
I was deeply troubled by high math
And such parables as the ark
And every beast in twos. One Saturday
I floated on an inner tube in a canal
And the best-looking girls at the end of our universe
Were on shore, peeling back
The wrappers of Butterfingers. Right there,
With sweetness greasing up their thighs,
I understood that I was too old to captain
An inner tube down a canal. I needed an ocean liner
On a sea splintered with sunlight,
Some stretch of watery romance. When I waved,
The girls barely looked
As I bobbed over the current.
The green cool water had shrunk my desire,
Thumb-long flesh just beginning to steer me wrong.

MAGAZINE ADVICE

It's staying light later, and through the pyracantha,
Through memory and its prickly blood,
A teenage boy combs his clean-cut hair,

A flood of rain water parting over his floppy shoes.
He shivers in his thin coat. Something has to happen
Because he has read in his sister's *Seventeen*
That if you wait long enough at a corner
The probability of a girl saying "hi"
Is stronger than a jet going down in a cow field.
He practices "hi" from 3:45 to 6:00
And jumps from foot to foot, his socks soaked,
His breath a white hovel for an angel.
He stands at the corner. Long cars pass,
The red coals of cigarettes in back seats.
A milk truck passes. Blue-haired widows pass.
A cloud that is the pinched face of W. C. Fields passes
And throws down a rag of water on some other part
Of town. But no girls venture in rain,
And right there, at the corners of Shame and Sadness,
The teenager turns and looks into a pyracantha bush —
A gardening glove lost among its thorns and thorny leaves.
Maybe for penance, for a motherly "I told you so,"
The boy shoves his hands among thorns when no girl appears.
Maybe he takes his hand home and soaks it in a pink basin.
Maybe he lifts a fork and eats because life goes on.
Maybe in bed his hand crawls into a pair of shorts,
The light of the day coming to an oily end.

NOT KNOWING

By then, by the time my brother
Was getting married, weeks before the old
Apartment was pulled down,
The evenings were warm and the sounds of
Freight trains absorbed by three oleanders,
Whipped by wind and iron clanging.
By then, by the time I was nineteen
And the crickets were hauling their armor
Into the weeds and dusty bushes,

I was thinking that I would have to read more.
I had to put together the meaning of our neighbors
Fighting in bed, then loving in bed from 3:30 to 4:00.
I would have to read more. My other neighbor
Had painted his porch light blue, and the first
Black family on our college-poor street
Were so friendly that they disturbed my views
About trust and mistrust. And I was stymied
When my brother and I tried
To remove the refrigerator
Down a narrow flight of steps.
Now it was stuck, lodged between
The walls, an absurd physics for the wrecking crew
To solve. The beast of machinery would start up
And the old apartment would come down
The weekend my brother would pin
A carnation to his lapel, the ruffle of petal
Perfuming the air as he walked down the aisle.
By then, by the time my brother was ready
And the refrigerator was leaking
Its gray liquids and gases,
I would sit my sorrow on a lawn,
Flattening the grass with the heel of my palm.
The grass springing back from this kind of pressure,
Another physics I couldn't figure on paper
Or a blackboard of low math. The spin
Of light and wind
And the residue
Of an exhausted star told me nothing.
After my brother was gone
I sat with a book on the lawn,
The evening blood-red in the west
And my palm pressing the balance of solitary grass,
The world of unknowable forces stirring
Every live and dead tree.

MAKING UP TIME
in memory of Ernesto Trejo

Leaves unfurled skyward from every living
And sick tree. The grass rippled
And fattened tomatoes cracked in glory.
We liked our summers. Both of us wore jeans
And plaid shirts, and our hair
Was just long enough to make us look like hippies.
The traffic of rusty Torinos moved our hair,
Traffic and sharp turns on poor streets.
We laughed at ourselves, and this too moved our hair.
We laughed as we recalled all-night diners and laundromats,
Both of us at heart merchants licking pencils
And adding up the day's earnings at night.
Surely if we got jobs, real ones,
We would please our wives with their buckled pots
And lapful of beans. We would please our mothers
Cutting dresses on the floor, needles glinting
In their mouths. We would make everyone happy
If a little crease of dirt and adult worry
Worked into our knuckles.

Instead, we dreamed up jobs while we walked.
When we turned a corner,
There were houses with blistered paint,
And behind the blisters
A scurry of ants searched for a living.
We could have learned from those ants.
We could have learned from family –
Barber who was your father, raisin mule who was mine.
We talked about work, the diner
By the freeway and the slow tumble of clothes
In our laundromats. We talked books by the armfuls –
The hero E sweeping a broom across the page,
And me with the worn elbows propping sadness

On a kitchen table.
Young, with new wives, we lived on very little.
Sparrows devoured sunlight and branch-scuffed fruit.
The lawns sprouted, where sprinklers hissed
From noon to nightfall. We turned a corner,
And our hair bounced. We laughed
By a canal, where lizards hugged the dusty shadows,
We sat with our hands on our knees.
In the distance,
A palm tree stood tall as a giraffe,
Drawing water in quick bursts through its long throat.
We were servants to trees and the heat-wavering valley,
And on that summer day we asked:
How could its leafy top frolic in wind
When the work of its root bore down through rock
And darkness, all for the apparent flow of youth.

PLANET NEWS

I feel for my car keys,
And touch the claw that lives inside a rabbit's foot,
Bite that reminds me that I am flesh.
I put on one shoe, then the next,
And for no reason I think of a Russian astronaut
And the full orbit that can bring out a beard
In less than a day. For all I know
He's tapping on his glass and looking down on us,
Along with God who has tired of our romance
And schemes for money.

Funny how the mind works.
It spins not unlike that astronaut,
His throat lined with the icy light of a comet,
Or like God, who weighs the apple

To the orange. I sigh
And I poke the cuff of my sweater,
Nibbled by a mouse that beds down in the wall.

I get up from my bed, sit back down.
I touch my tie with its anchor that weighs the heart.
At the window, I look skyward
Where the astronaut is smoothing his ancient beard.
God, I see, is bringing out his book,
His tongue black from licking his pencil
Again and again.

SIZING UP A MARRIAGE

After Mexico, we lived on oranges,
It seemed, some laughter,
Some friendship that knocked
A clean knuckle at the door.
The winter sky gave up
Nothing, not rain
Or a leaflet of work.
Having none, we thought of money,
And drew pictures at the kitchen
Table. We were artists, me with
My dog-exercising machine,
And you with Asian pasta
Rolled on a wooden paddle.
What did we know, poor
And newly married? My shirts
Were ironed, my three pairs
Of pants pressed
And folded two ways in
My drawer. I was writing
About small people breaking
Into houses, their fat knees

Scrubbing the rug when
The police passed. I was eating
Those oranges by the twos and threes,
The sweet acid rolling off
My fingers. Winter rolled over
Wires and telephone poles
And the valley fog ate up
Every car and bum dripping
In gray rags. We stayed
In our house, the floor furnace
Ticking. When the telephone
Rang, we jumped, both hungry
For news. Once, when I had
To drive my loneliness
To a river, I went outside
And discovered a man
Perched on the car fender,
His gray pants flapping in wind.
"What are you doing" I snapped.
He pointed and said he was looking
Over his life — an ex-wife
In a faraway apartment
And kids in every dirty window.
After he ran away, I climbed to look
At marriage two flights up —
Radio on and no one singing.

WATER AND LIGHT
for Carolyn

It's alright to rake up
An inch of hard earth,
To set a sprinkler
On a backyard patch,
And to lean on that rake

And think of the future
That breathes water and light,
Some small flickering roots.
And after this dirt was crumbled
And let loose its anger,
It's alright to toss
A handful of feathery seed,
And follow the flight
Of a bird from a fence
To the clothesline,
Where my jeans weep soapy tears.
It's alright to want grass,
To lay facing a single star,
Some cloud that raked
The Pacific. Love, all summer
You were water and light,
And, at night, the silky dent
That brings a man to his wasted knees.

FAIR TRADE

I did my best when I was young,
Just married, just walking my love
From one room to the next.
I was living in my madness —
The traffic inside
My head while outside
Our downtown apartment, *vatos*
Cruised with blue tattoos ...
I walked my wife from
One sun-lit room to the next,
And on a dead Sunday
I walked her to the Azteca Cafe,
Slum eating, rags
Of chicken wings, lumpy gravy,

The anemic coins
Of carrots. My money,
Then, was dollar bills
That tumbled through the wash
And coins warmed by sunlight
On the chest of drawers.
Money is what gave me
A plate of chicken,
Steam like a glove,
And when I wiped
My glasses, a Mexican man
Was asking for toast.
The waitress turned
And started the order,
Two slices browning
In their stand-up bed
Of red, angry filaments.
When she said, "Dollar thirty,"
I thought, two slices
No meat or butter. The man
Hesitated, then fumbled for
Coins from his pocket.
This, I saw, was pride.
I stabbed my carrots,
Hurting for this man.
He took his toast
In a napkin,
Toast that was already cool.
He left no trail of crumbs
But the line of memory
From my eye to the bell jingling
On the closing door.

SOME COINS

Now and then I punched
A hand into my pocket
And fingered a dime or a quarter
And couldn't remember how
It got there, this money,
This wafer of light
And promise. Now and then
I flipped coins
With my uncle, the one
With a spade of Chinese hair
On his chin and a shiny space
Where horns might go.
He let me win.
I got on my bike
And rode madly
Confounded by my luck
And the ho-ho laughter of
Uncle eagerly giving up coins.
I stopped my bike when glitter
Caught my eye – cellophane
Or foil gum wrappers,
Camel-back nails,
The overturned crowns
Of bottle caps.
I was out to make a living,
Eyes scouring the streets.
I was out to pick up
The dime with a beard of grit,
Buffalo nickel, and smashed penny,
And the quarter tapped by a spoon
Into a junior-high ring.
In one wild turn
Of corner, I caught sight
Of my grandfather
Leaving the barbershop,

Patting his back pocket
For his wallet tooled
With an Aztec calendar.
I rolled to a stop.
I stared at the silver dollar
Pressed into his belt buckle.
I loved that belt buckle,
That silver dollar and halo of pesos.
Once, Grandpa took off his belt
When for fun I knocked plums
Off his tree and he ran after me.
It was the only time
Money ever chased me around.

OLD HOUSE IN MY FORTIETH YEAR

The clod's stubbornness gives in to my fist.
The snail groans a single bubble under my shoe.
The roots of every chinaberry I've swung from
Needle even further into the moist earth.
I'm home in these weeds. I'm home in these bones,
This flesh with its laughter and fatherly scent,
Flesh held up by a frayed belt on its last hole.
I don't have to walk far to hear the jay
Or a vicious dog, a coal breathing in each eye.

The old house has been smoothed by sand
And the rake of years. I don't know this place,
Really, or the boy buried in this flesh of mine.
One error, and I'm the man pushing a cart.
Another error, and I march a long row of cotton
Or beets. The stars wheeled around an icy comet,
And by fortune, I'm now at home in this body –
The heart down to business
And slapping blood through its swinging door.

WATERWHEEL

I sat with slivers of foxtails in each sock
And a stick that stirred rainwater,
Gush of a cloud that passed over our house.
I was five, and it was five in the afternoon,
Spring I guess. The mailman had come and gone
On his bicycle, his pants gnashed in the oily chain.
The diesels had stopped. The whistle at Sun-Maid Raisin
Had cleared the air. Men the color of sparrows
Had walked home, father among them, all tired
And swinging their lunch pails like lanterns.
I was coming alive. Sure, I was cold,
And my shoes were curled. Sure, my hair was wet
And I was beginning to shiver. But I was waiting
For Arnold, a boy up the alley. He promised
Me the Chinese garden in a clam shell –
Waterwheel, bridge, and a woman with a fan,
Quiet beauty on a street stomped all night by machinery.
I waited with rain on my eyelashes.
Fortune was mine. After all, hadn't I raced my bicycle
Under a moving diesel? Hadn't I pushed myself
Hand over fist on the telephone wire?
I waited for the Chinese garden
And its waterwheel to turn in the long life of rain.

AFTERNOON MEMORY

Sometimes I'll look in the refrigerator
And decide that the mustard is vaguely familiar,
And that the jar of Spanish olives is new to me.
What's this gathering? The butter
And salsa, the two kinds of tortillas
And, in back, the fat-waisted Mrs. Butterworth.
I'll study the plate of cross-legged chicken,

And close the refrigerator and lean on the kitchen counter.
Is this old age? The faucet drips.
The linoleum blisters when you walk on it.
The magnets on the refrigerator crawl down
With the gravity of expired coupons and doctor bills.
Sometimes I'll roll my tongue in my mouth.
Is this thirst or desire? Is this pain
Or my foot going to sleep? I know the factory
Inside my stomach has gone quiet.
My hair falls as I stand. My lungs are bean plants
Of disappearing air. My body sends signals, like now:
A healthy fleck is floating across my vision.
I watch it cross. It's going to attack a virus
On the right side of my body
And, later, travel down my throat to take care of knee,
Little latch of hurt. I swallow three times.
I have to help my body parts. Fellas, sour liver
And trusty kidney, I'm full of hope.
I open the refrigerator.
I've seen this stuff before. What's this?
The blow dart of bran? Chinese ginger?
No, fellas, they're carrots. The orange, I hear,
Is good for your eyes.

A BETTER VIEW

The nail was a camel hump in wood,
But sharp when you climbed onto the roof
To get a better view of your place,
Your hometown, maybe a husband and wife
Shoveling spring bulbs in the back yard,
Maybe a squirrel polishing its teeth on a walnut,
Or the pinwheel of hope and dizzy flush of clean air,
Blue in the hoop, a handle on the earth.
The nail cut into your finger,

A laughing mouth of blood spilling.
Without thinking, you shoved this slash
Into your mouth and tasted this salty laughter.
You dropped from the roof and looked at it –
Gill of rusty hurt,
Flap of sting and scolding "I told you so."
When you opened it,
You saw the red that flexes the heart
And cradles the lung. You cradled your finger
And hurried home,
One drop falling in the dust,
The other onto your flopping shoe.
All you wanted was a better view –
Glimpse of the water tower and tall factory,
The kind of beauty that shimmers on a pool in summer.
But God was finishing his horde of apples
When he looked down and saw you, ten year old.
He wiped his fingers on his sleeve
And made the nail, that camel hump, rise up
From the tarred shingles
And strike you before you saw too much
Of a world truant with disease.

SATURDAY IN CHINATOWN
for Shorty Cruz

I walked backward on my heels
And fed the meter two more bright pennies.
I caught up with my uncle, the Marine,
And for every one of his steps
I was taking three,
My arms pulled in like wings
And churning a pant
From the deepest folds of lung.
On Saturday, Chinatown was a hive of
Shoppers, the slaughter of meat

In windows, the call of shoeshine
And newspaper boy with his pitch of war
And capsized ships. Back then
It was the whistle of sailors
From land-locked Nebraska, the clang of trains
Unloading at Southern Pacific.
It was the merchants behind
The pyramids of three kinds of apples.
It was Armenian men slapping tobacco
From their trousers. It was Japanese
And Mexican, Chinese with blue bundles
Under their arms. It was chickens
In a wire cage. I stared at one
Chicken, and it stared back.
I walked at my uncle's strong side,
Dressed in my barber shirt
Sporting stitched-on scissors and comb,
My toy magnifying glass
Heating the back of my right hand.
My pockets rattled with marbles
And bottle caps, a roll of caps,
A foxtail that was a jet fighter.
I was putting the world to use,
And every now and then I would reach down
And try to pull the comb from
My shirt. But it was stitched there,
A snaggle of thread coming loose.
More than once, I thought of lowering my head
And running my hair over this comb.
I was four, maybe five. My shoe laces
Were a tangle of knots.
I was living mostly by the judgments
My tongue made and a few hurts,
A scab on my knee, the front tooth
With a corner gone out. It was
Saturday. I was looking around
With a magnifying glass, my eye
Burning up the world.

I'm in a hotel where you take out
Your own trash – one tea bag,
Lemon wedge of squeezed life,
Apple core, Kleenex with three tears.
I'm unhappy watching rain
From a third floor, and sick,
A stab in my throat when I swallow.
I cough, I blow my nose.
I don't have time to lie with my hands
On my chest, quite dead.
I make my bed, wash my cup and plate.
I dust two tragic books, smooth the bed,
And shake an ant from my bananas.
I flush the toilet to be sure
And rinse my shaver, reckless skate
That stopped too close to my nose.
I sit in a chair, wait,
And watch the ant stagger through the carpet.
Then, a bang at the door, jingle of keys,
And something like a scary dream comes in:
The biggest maid in Ohio.
Her apron like a single flake of confetti
On her belly. I'm like that ant – frail.
She doesn't look at me. She goes
To the bathroom and fingers my towels,
Says, They're good for two more days.
I ask, What about my sheets?
She pushes me aside,
And says, You too skinny to stink
100% American cotton. She bangs the door
Closed and I sit at my table.
I'm far from home, poor. The ant is poor
Without its family of bananas,
The black sugar spots and greasy peel.
Brotherly mercy at this table. I crack the banana,
One half for him, one half for me,

And we lower our mandibles
Into this sturdy and ancient mush.

SUPER-EIGHT MOVIES

By noon the shadows crawl
Into the trees, where they'll remain
Until half-past three. The dog whines
From his chain. The children who crowned
Each other with plastic baseball bats have gone inside,
The fever of play in their pink skin.
TV helps, I suppose, hours of
Snowy TV and Kool-Aid in blue aluminum tumblers.
Mother of all butt whippings hides
Behind a damp wash cloth, shoes kicked off.
Her neck is pleated; crazy hair
Smothers her armpits. Her cat,
By all signs, is deaf to the three flies
Kicking their legs idiotically in a water bowl.

So. So as Fresno flops on its daily sorrows,
Jon and I sketch our movies on yellow paper.
We're waiting for our leading lady
Sitting on the toilet, lid down,
Powdering the good side
Of her nose. We can't start
Without sorrow, waste, and sadness,
The world without a tattered, ballroom gown.
When I tiptoe at the window and say,
It's time, sweetie,
She yells with a comb in her hair,
Shut the fuck up!

We laugh off our boredom.
I pick up our borrowed camera

And give it a good wind. I can't start
With happiness first. I say
Jon, think of thirst, power, and a good job.
A pro from way back, Jon picks up the garden hose,
Drinks, and backhands water from his chin.
The camera rattles its WWII sprockets
And jumps like a chicken in my hands.
That's good! I holler. Gimme a surprised look.
Jon lifts his eyebrows and grins
All the way to the tops of his gums.
Sweat, like ambition, comes racing out.

SUMMER MARRIAGE
for Jon Veinberg

Rage is a pay cut for the same work,
A stripped bolt
And motor oil leaking into your one good eye.

The fan belt hanging from a dog's mouth.
The white root poking through clay plumbing
And the toilet backing up,
A flood of skunk water hitting the tile floor.

Rage is the snowy TV,
The blistered thumb frozen to empty ice cube tray.

The birth of five kittens in a detergent box
A parrot spitting seed at its shiny bell.
The child's crying hatred for his eyeless teddy.

Through all this,
Through the day that was a hammer of heat,
I'm happy with my iced tea and slaughtered lemon.
So is my friend, swallowing slivers of ice.
It's hot somewhere inside our river

Of blood. It's hot and we're too close to argue.
We're letting our neighbors do this for us.

The wife stomps down the steps,
This time with only one suitcase,
Handle torn and carrying it like a child.
Last week she had two suitcases and a shoulder bag.
This week perhaps there is less to carry away,
A few dresses and scraped-to-their-nails shoes.
The screen door slams,
And I slam a gnat in my ear,
A cause and effect on a hot night
When every third house breaks into a vicious sweat.

BOOKS BY GARY SOTO

New and Selected Poems

Jesse

Pieces of the Heart

Home Course in Religion

A Summer Life

Who Will Know Us?

Lesser Evils

California Childhood

Small Faces

Living Up the Street

Black Hair

Where Sparrows Work Hard

The Tale of Sunlight

The Elements of San Joaquin